SELLING THE *RIGHT* WAY

Choosing Your Path to Improved Sales Outcomes

MIKE CONNOLLY

Copyright © 2017 Mike Connolly

All rights reserved.

No part of this work may be reproduced, or stored in a retrieval system, or transmitted in any form or by any means, electronic, mechanical, photocopying, recording, or otherwise without written permission of the author.

ISBN: 978-1546868286

IN DEDICATION TO MY WIFE
for supporting me throughout my career
and sharing the achievements in our life.

NOTE TO READER

THE STORIES, names, and circumstances in this book come from more than 30 years of my experience in selling, sales leadership, sales operations, and executive leadership. The names and details have been altered to protect those involved while staying true to the lesson learned. It is these lessons that led to my personal success. While I cannot guarantee readers the same results, I can attest that my success was a direct result of the methodologies and philosophies discussed in this book.

A bit about myself: throughout my 30-year career, I have worked with organizations ranging from small startups to Fortune 500-based customers across a wealth of industries—financial, healthcare, pharmaceutical, manufacturing, public sector, retail, and more. Throughout those years I have been responsible for selling or leading sales related to products, services—including outsourcing, managed services, consulting, call-center, professional services, and staffing services—and cloud-based technologies. The majority of my years were focused on a wide array of selling in the field of technology.

My methods and principles for achieving sales success were created with a focus on sales enablement and productivity as a whole, not specific to any individual industry or area of specialization. Regardless of what you sell, they will improve your business outcomes.

Win, Succeed and Have Fun!

CONTENTS

CHAPTER 1: Introduction 1
Selling for Maximum Outcomes

CHAPTER 2: Ask Yourself the Big Question 11
Then Never Stop Asking

CHAPTER 3: Relationship Selling or Bust 17
It's Not Me, It's You...That Matters

CHAPTER 4: The Value of the Right Focus and Right Quality 29
Creating Outcomes from Consistency

CHAPTER 5: The Right Company Makes a Major Difference 43
Make It a Match for Greatest Outcomes

CHAPTER 6: Start with the Right Strategic Plan 59
Planning for the Highest Business Outcomes

CHAPTER 7: The Right Mindset 79
You Can Achieve When You Believe

CHAPTER 8: The Right Leadership to Maximize Your Outcomes 97
The Value of Leadership that Leads from the Front

CHAPTER 9: The Right People Make a World of Difference 109
Changing Business Outcomes by Hiring for Results

CHAPTER 10: Combining Plans and People with the Right Customers...127
Aim for the Bottom, Get the Bottom; Aim for the Top, Win

CHAPTER 11: Positioning the Right Solution Offering 143
Matching Right Value with Need Rarely Loses

CHAPTER 12: Right Relationships Accelerate Success............155
Relationships Can Help Grow or Slow

CHAPTER 13: Get Your Sales Funnel Right............161
Right Opportunities Matter for Best Success

CHAPTER 14: The Right Quota or Budget............173
Accelerators or Inhibitors?

CHAPTER 15: Build a Culture That's Right for You............219
Best Outcomes Come from Best Attitudes

CHAPTER 16: The Time is Right Now............231
Success That Waits Is Success Lost

CHAPTER 17: Reaping the Benefits from the Right Results............237
A Lifetime of Success

CHAPTER 18: Your New Path to Improving Success............243
Turning Lessons into Practice

Chapter 1

INTRODUCTION
Selling for Maximum Outcomes

THIRTY YEARS INTO MY CAREER, I still consider sales the best possible career path I could have chosen. I truly believe that no other career could have been as rewarding, both financially and personally, for me. I also know it was the career that best aligned with my personality, skills, and the natural instincts that help us as individuals reach our goals. None of this is to say that I haven't experienced challenges throughout my career, but those opportunities enabled me to reach a higher level of business outcome and success. Let me state early on that my success came from my clear understanding that sales were not about what was in it for me: sales are, and always have been, about how to understand what is in it for my customers. I care every day about what I can do to increase customer intimacy, create a high-level customer experience, and strengthen overall customer loyalty. As you read this book, note how the ideas I share can benefit your customer, not your earnings. When you view the world through that lens your selling success can and will be unlimited, as will your ability to achieve greater earnings potential. I often say that when it comes to P&L management, as long as we care for the customers and our employees to the best of our ability, the numbers will fall into place.

Since I have already used the words *success* and *choice* several times in my first paragraph, let's clarify them. Success comes in many forms and means something different to everyone. I feel that the use of the word success is not specific to financial achievement—contrary to what one might assume about a person in a sales career. I look for success in individual accomplishments, the achievement of defined personal goals or milestones, the ability to attain company-defined expectations, my ability to earn a promotion or next step in my career, and of course, financial stability for my family. (Of course, writing this book has been another type of accomplishment—and a truly rewarding one!) My keys to success are deeply personal, and I'm sure you have a list of those that make you successful as well.

My use of the word choice here and on the cover means, specifically, that success is a choice. It is something you decide to achieve, something that depends entirely on how you choose to handle all the elements of your sales career approach. Elements such as the company you work for, the products you sell, your individual selling method, and the customers you work with have to be properly selected to maximize your ability to achieve success. They have to be right. My choices were my commitment to the **rights** you will read about later in this book. My methods allowed me to define the choices that led to my success and not allow success to choose me.

> **My methods allowed me to define the choices that led to my success and not allow success to choose me.**

I once had a psychologist ask me the question "How will you know when you get there"? *There*, of course, meant success—the things we strive for in our career. I honestly did not have an answer. She had asked it, she explained, because I seemed always striving for something. Between my working long hours to advance my career and completing my MBA as an adult student, she felt there must be some concrete goal I was reaching for. So how would I know when I reached it?

It was a thought-provoking moment for me, and an uncomfortable one—uncomfortable because I had no answer at the time. I knew I had achieved many things throughout my career both personally and professionally, yet I continued to strive for more. I took a long time to internalize the question, and it soon became apparent that my only real reason for striving for more was because I could. As new opportunities presented themselves, I simply said yes; I was making mechanical decisions rather than choices based on aspirations and goals. Today, when something new presents itself, I ask myself the question to ensure it is a choice I make, not a direction I simply follow.

I encourage you to consider this question for yourself to ensure that you are putting the right amount of effort into the right places in your career. While exactly what I am striving for may always be evolving, I am comfortable in my many achievements thus far in my career, and know that I am headed in the right direction. I know in my heart that if my career came to a close today, I would be pleased with what I have accomplished.

Like many who work in sales, I began my career with a desire to earn money. The drive started not with my first corporate job, but years earlier—with my first paper route, at the age of 13. Per the newspaper company policy, customers were allowed to pay for the paper I delivered, but only if they wanted to. Imagine that? Whether you paid or not, you still received the paper twice a week at your home. Even at an early age I knew that to make people want to pay when they were not required to do so, I would have to make them feel that they were receiving a benefit from my way of delivering the paper. I realized that the way to their happiness was personal convenience from the service I provided.

I set one objective for myself: I would make sure every paper was delivered next to their front door. Not their driveway, their lawn, or even the lowest step on their porch—but in that sweet spot where they only had to open their door, lean over, and pick it up. I focused my throwing skills each day I delivered, and whenever the paper took an unwanted detour into the bushes, I took the time to retrieve it and ensure it was on the doorstep within reach. My belief even at age 13 was that I could only earn their loyalty and satisfaction by making things convenient for them; then they would be more accepting to pay for the service, not the paper.

Well, nearly every customer paid. One customer even told me, "I want to pay for this paper because of how much I appreciate the pride you take in delivering it to my door. You do a really good job." Hearing that statement validated what I had hoped would be the outcome. My success in accomplishing my goal led to my being recognized as the top earner for my paper route, and I won a trip...to the movies. More importantly in my mind, other paper delivery people recognized me as the top earner, and thus I received the recognition I quickly realized I enjoyed. My pay for delivering the papers did not change, but my sense of accomplishment increased dramatically. I was hooked. This was the beginning of my interest in roles where I could receive recognition for my work and for making others happy. The feeling was exhilarating!

On the first day of freshman baseball practice in high school (go Tigers!), the coach informed us that each player had to sell 30 seat cushions emblazoned with the school logo so that we could buy a new pitching machine for the team. With nothing but a signup sheet and no sample product to show prospective customers, my friend and I went door to door that very first night. He worked one side of the street and I worked the other. I sold 59 that first night. This was good old-fashioned door-to-door selling, not my parents taking the sheet to their office or standing in front of the supermarket like so many students do today! I could not have been more proud of myself when the coach announced my results the next afternoon. Most of my teammates had not even started yet; I already stood at the top of the stack rankings. (Well, stack rankings did not really exist back then, but we all know the feeling.) I trace my ability to overachieve in sales to those early years feeling of accomplishment and by the time I began my career was confident my skills and understanding of sales would make me successful.

Eventually I accepted my first corporate sales job. This first taste of sales was all I needed to know that I could do great things. As a telemarketer, I made a minimal pay by selling daily letter pack pickups for Purolator Courier, a competitor of Federal Express, Airborne and UPS. I was told on my first day that the minimum quota to earn commission was to sell 5 weekly pickups and 25 one-time pickups per week. If I did that, I would make a commission of $5 for each pickup beyond that minimum requirement. The other sellers, confiding in me over the cubicle walls, told me that it would be tough to reach that goal initially but that over time I would be able to make some extra money through commissions. As in all typical sales organizations, there was a big whiteboard on the front wall where each seller's results were tracked so that everyone could see who was leading in sales for the week (as well as who was at the bottom of the list).

I sat at my desk and immediately began making calls to potential customers who had filled out index card surveys from mailers, magazines, and handouts. Looking back, it was like the gold leads in the movie *Glengarry Glen Ross*; the other sellers were so excited to receive their fresh batch of cards and begin making outbound calls. I recall finishing a call that first morning and asking loud enough for all to hear: "How do I enter a new pickup in the computer"? Everyone stopped what they were doing and looked at me in amazement. I was the new guy with one of the first sales of the day; that likely put a lot of pressure on the experienced reps. At the conclusion of the first week, my name was in the number two spot. I could hear people whispering to one another that my sales were due to the good leads I had rather than my skills, but I knew better.

The following week in our Monday morning sales meeting, the corporate head of sales—who was apparently rarely seen—came down from his office and asked: "Which of you is Mike Connolly?" When I raised my hand he walked over, shook it, congratulated me, and asked if I could repeat what I had done the prior week.

I gave him a big smile and said, as boldly as I could manage, "I can do better. That was pretty easy."

I'm sure I did not earn any friends in the sales department that morning, but I was ready to make myself known. I continued to show up on the big whiteboard in first and second place for many months to come. The adrenaline of a win was worth it.

I learned quickly the approach that worked best for me and applied it daily to my calling efforts. I began by focusing on large corporations where I could easily schedule weekly pickups while also setting up daily trials for smaller departments. This reduced my number of calls yet increased my opportunity to expand the number of pickups per call. It also gave me the opportunity to turn those smaller department trials into weekly pickups at a later date.

My entry into a sales career quickly taught me that becoming more efficient in my sales approach had numerous benefits, as highlighted in Table 1.

TABLE 1: BENEFITS

COMPANY BENEFITS	PERSONAL BENEFITS
Company earned more revenue	Job security
Customer satisfaction increased	Improved career path
Culture within my company improved	Financial security for my family
Creating repeat customers	Increased earnings
I earned higher respect from my peers and leadership	Personal satisfaction/pride

I was reaching the success all sellers and sales leaders strive to attain. Even better, I was not doing so through a random approach to selling; I was beginning to create my own winning formula to successful selling that fit my personal style.

Don't get me wrong, I worked a lot of hours—and I do mean ***a lot!*** I have always felt working 9-5 will result in good pay, but to be at the top 5% of the team in sales, you have to put in the time and effort and not count the hours within a day. Each day my failures became a valuable asset to my success as I learned from each. Meanwhile, my repeated successes only solidified my belief that my sales modeling and approach were beginning to mold into a formula that worked well for me.

However, further growth and success were always on my mind. As the years passed I worked with many different companies, primarily within the technology sector. At different intervals, I sold offerings that included software, computers, networking, data center, call center, security, managed services, outsourcing, and more. Those technologies that embody the IT infrastructure of a company. Yet with every company and business offering, I strategically found ways to make the most out of every appointment with my customers. Once I moved into a sales leadership role, my adrenaline picked up. Now I had the ability not only to influence my individual base of customers, but to expand my strategies as part of the daily actions of the entire sales team. That's when selling really became exciting: The success I recognized as an individual contributor suddenly expanded exponentially as I helped many people experience similar success. My enjoyment of sales now sprung from more than just individual achievement and financial fulfillment. I was opening a door into what I came to enjoy the most: strategy and planning for a team.

It was becoming clearer than ever that when I focused my choices on a defined strategy, my outcomes improved. More specifically, as I focused my choices on those areas that most greatly impacted my ability to be successful, both my and my team's success grew. Just as important, the more I focused my choices on the benefits to the customer, the more customers wanted to deal only with my company and not my competitors. The customers were telling me with their actions that they wanted to work with a person or company who understood their business better and spent more time working with them. They wanted a higher level of intimacy with their seller, and I was more than happy to accept that responsibility.

Sales and sales leadership can be highly rewarding if you follow a philosophy you truly believe in. When you do so, you are rewarded in turn for your efforts. Identifying your strengths and committing to your success plan is an important facet of your ability to achieve success consistently. Rewards come in many forms: a higher quality of life, customer relationships, corporate respect, increased confidence

Chapter 2

ASK YOURSELF THE BIG QUESTION
Then Never Stop Asking

IF YOU PLAN TO SPEND YOUR CAREER AND LIFE SELLING, you need to know with conviction the answer to the following question: "Is sales right for me, and am I right for sales?" The second part to that question is important to know as you read this book. Of the many rights I discuss that lead to your success in sales, you will only be positively impacted if you yourself are right for sales. Sales is not a halfway commitment if you truly want to reach higher goals. Those who want to work just hard enough to earn a paycheck will eventually be weeded out by natural selection in many business environments. Trust me when I say that sales can he incredibly fun, and when you win the feeling is euphoric; but as you will experience throughout your selling career, wins can occur less often than losses, and the losses hurt five times as much. It is often not just a bruised ego; it's the kind of hurt you can take emotionally. Losses can lead yourself to question your own ability, can result in leadership asking why you lost (which can be exhausting), and can put stress on your ability to support your family. The hurt is real and not for the faint of heart. So being honest with who you are inside and knowing that you can mentally and physically overcome the ebbs and flows that sales smacks you with on a daily basis is important.

A career in sales is truly not for everyone, and many intelligent and capable people have tried and failed. For a large majority, the losses that are so frequent early in a career are too much to overcome psychologically. Fortunately, some of those who fail early are able to chart a new course for their intended career before they get too involved in a career they do not truly enjoy. Others seem to pull the Band Aid of failure off slowly, just hoping the pain might go away. Those people suffer from a lack of being honest with themselves and recognizing that sales is not the most effective career path for them. This lack of self-awareness can lead to wasted time for those who do not have the talent or passion to make sales their career.

It is possible to make money in sales even if you are not passionate about it, but not to attain the level of success people who truly enjoy it experience. And in any case, the level of financial reward simply does not make up for the pain of enduring a career you do not enjoy. I am not advising that you quit sales if you are unsure about your level of commitment, but I am recommending that you be honest with yourself early enough in your career to determine the best choices for you. *Early* is relative here; a career can be 40 or more years. Make the choice that will make you happiest.

When reading this book, you need to know *you* to help make a better you in a selling environment. Knowing you means understanding what makes you passionate, what matters most to you in your work, and how to maximize your strengths and limit your weaknesses to best place you in a position to be not just successful, but happy. We all have weaknesses, but honestly recognizing what they are to help you avoid pitfalls is critically important in a sales career. The best sellers and sales leaders are incredibly self-aware and use that knowledge to overcome their shortcomings.

If you want to win more frequently and increase your ability to be successful, identify your weakness and make it a strength. You can do this through training or skills improvement or by aligning yourself with someone on your team with that strength to assist on the deal. Forget ego and pride; there is no pride in losing because you won't ask for assistance from someone with more experience or skills in a certain area. Be honest with yourself and sales will truly be a fulfilling career choice.

Let's conduct a good yet simple self-awareness exercise right now that will benefit you throughout the remainder of this book. Take the time to answer these three questions, and be as honest as you can.

1. **What am I really good at doing in sales or sales leadership?**
    Some examples of answers:
    a. I am a better farmer than hunter.
    b. I am strong at networking.
    c. Creating presentations and then presenting is a skill of mine.
2. **What do I know is a weakness or makes me uncomfortable?**
    Some examples of answers:
    a. Describing our solution in detail makes me uncomfortable.
    b. Negotiations make me nervous.
    c. If someone says no, I never know how to react.

3. **What would I consider an unknown, or a skill that I'm not sure is a strength or weakness yet?**
   Some examples of answers:
   a. I have never done a cold call, so I am not sure if I am good at it.
   b. I have never negotiated a deal with a customer. I'm not sure I have the strength to do so or not.
   c. I get nervous speaking with people about prices. I hope to overcome that over time.

This exercise is a useful measurement of how you think about yourself. Creating these lists now will enable you to reassess your answers as you progress through the book. I would also take the time while reading to move answers, if necessary, as you experience self-awareness moments. Take the opportunity to write these thoughts down as they come to mind. The value of the exercise lies in being honest now, before you are unable or unwilling to recognize an area for improvement or support and thus put your career at risk. Know as well that what you document in your list as a weakness *can* become a strength over time if you are committed to improving it; there are plenty of options available to help you improve these skills. However, if you know with certainty that you have weaknesses you will never overcome due to fear or a total lack of enjoyment, then step back and consider your options now before you get too deep.

Throughout my career I have had to address my weaknesses, and I still do. I know I am a person who is more confident in a deeper more granular discussion than a broader overview of products. Luckily, this often caused my customers to see me as not just a basic salesperson, but someone who was passionate about what they sold and a person they could trust and respect. However, it could cause a problem when working with minor details and specifics. When I sold software, I had to take the time to learn the many layers of the product and work hard on my ability to demo every area and understand how it applied to make the customer better. More specifically, how that function or capability supported the need of the customer and was a true benefit for them. I did the same early in my career with networking. I studied the guides, took certifications, and set up all aspects of the network myself so that I could experience what the customers were experiencing. I even had the technical team crash the network so I could try and fix the issue. Am I stating you have to do the same to make you successful? No. My point is that I knew my own weakness was improved by my taking steps I knew would boost my confidence level. Just focus on what makes you better.

As you continue to read, you will see that my personal achievements have been driven by my understanding of how customers, focus, quality, consistency, and having fun would lead to my success. However, had I not been passionate about my career in sales or honest with who I am and my talents and shortcomings, I would not have had the ability to remain focused or provide quality. The very fact that I was confident in my sales roles enabled me to be comfortable in my skills and capabilities when with customers or my sales teams. This absolutely led to my being able to relax enough to trust my approach and apply the right level of focus and quality. My personal choices became more clear and applied with confidence. Had I not been able to achieve my level of confidence early in my career and sustain it, I can guarantee that I would not have had any fun—and if you are not having fun, why do it? A career is a long time to suffer if you do not enjoy the day-to-day aspects of your work.

That really is the essence of the book and what I share. The methods and principles that made me successful in my career can only achieve best results if you are honest about your strengths and weaknesses. From that awareness you will be able to begin to define all the rights I describe throughout the book in a way that maximizes your strengths, diminishes your weaknesses, and helps you achieve success.

Let me close this chapter with the same important question I posed in the beginning: "Is sales right for me, and am I right for sales?" Never stop asking and never stop improving, so that you can always be confident in how you respond.

Chapter 3

RELATIONSHIP SELLING OR BUST
It's Not Me, It's You...That Matters

"**S**TRIVE NOT TO BE A SUCCESS, but rather to be of value," said Albert Einstein. Let me get right to the point of this chapter and state point blank that if you got into a sales career purely to make money, go find a job recruiter, because your success in sales will be limited. The sooner you allow yourself that wisdom, the sooner you will be able to accelerate your sales career success.

Remember that old breakup line "It's not you, it's me"? George Costanza used it in *Seinfeld*, and unfortunately for him, it became an indicator of his identity. George struggled to maintain any type of love interest because he always thought only about how the relationship could benefit him, not about how it could benefit the woman he was dating. Even his use of "It's not you, it's me" was a way for him to avoid having women hate him when the breakup was final. He walked away guilt-free and satisfied that his own needs were met, not giving the slightest thought to the fact that this was a complete lie.

In all aspects of my sales career, I have focused on making the relationship with my customer the priority, not my own potential for reward. Unlike George Costanza, I looked at the customer and thought, "It's not about me; this is about you." Even when I had to say no to a customer, I knew that the no was in their best interest. It was that mentality that enabled me to fully embrace the idea that every call or meeting was an opportunity to make the customer feel like the most important individual in this relationship. I still advise my teams and consulting clients that when you focus your efforts on customer needs and provide them a value based on quality of your service, the financial outcome will take care of itself. Along these lines, and just as important, is the idea that you need not sell when building a relationship with a customer. The sale will be a result of how you effectively bond with and treat the customer.

Many books and articles have been written on the subject of relationship selling, and I have no plans to cover what so many have already so eloquently written on the subject. However, I want to discuss relationship selling briefly so you understand how the relationship sale was critical to my success and how the rights of this book are achieved. In my career the best relationships I have built were built on *trust, respect, communication, and caring*. Don't kid yourself: the customer knows you are a seller, and many people have a negative attitude toward sellers from the start. They fear the worst about sellers' promises; they believe sellers only want one thing from them (hint: it rhymes with *honey*). There's nothing like meeting a prospective customer for the first time, shaking their hand, and having that hanging over your head, right? Well, learn to get over

> *The best relationships I have built were built on trust, respect, communication, and caring.*

it quickly. Most of all, learn not to embody that stereotypical image of a seller the customer has built in their head. The best sellers in any business or industry are the best at relationship selling, not sales.

The bottom line is that customers want to know they can trust their salesperson. In other words, they want to know they can count on you. Remember, the decision that customer makes about their vendor will likely be due to the trust and respect they build with that individual; they will not take a risk, because by doing so they can put their own career at risk. Keep that in mind when working with your customers. Their job could be at risk every time you tell them a little white lie, overcommit, or under-deliver. Their initial negative feeling about you is not really about you—it has more to do with past sellers who did not deliver and their own fear related to the risks of losing their job. What is the best way to put them at ease? Earn their trust and respect every day, and let them know that you care more about them than you care about your next paycheck. They need to count on you like your family and friends count on you.

Show them respect and you will earn their respect. Customers should always feel it is about them; even if you have to say no, make it clear that no may in fact be in their best interest. Customers respect the hell out of a seller who is not simply a yes man, but demonstrates that the customer comes first. It is not always easy telling a customer that your company is not the best at providing a certain service due to it not currently being within your company's portfolio of capabilities. Far too many sellers are compelled to answer yes in fear of losing a deal, even when the company they represent does not even offer that service. Selling something you push your company to create on the fly more often than not leads to negative ramifications for you and your customer. When it fails, you immediately become the type of seller they feared from the beginning. Do not let the pressure of a sale deter you from what you know is best for the customer, especially with competitors and commission lurking. I have never lost a relationship due to my honesty—only strengthened it. A great way to avoid competitive influence is your own knowledge of the industry. Recommend a company you know or partner with for a need you cannot fulfill, and take control of whom the customer speaks with. Customers will respect you for doing so and appreciate your making their need to find further assistance an easier process. You retain control, as well as their respect and trust.

One of the worst things sales leaders and executives force sellers to do is push a customer to cut a PO because it is the end of a month, quarter, or fiscal year. While I truly do appreciate that money from closing a deal at the end of a period may be needed to achieve a budget or demonstrate performance to executives, the mere gesture of pushing a customer completely weakens any relationship building the seller has done for months, if not years. The relationship sale is not about getting a PO by the end of the month from that customer; it is based on the trust and respect the seller shows in trying to help the customer improve their business. Creating cracks in the customer's trust changes the customer's perception of the seller, and may even open the door to competitors. I consider that push for PO three steps forward (relationship selling) then two steps back (PO request perceived as seller wants commission); it does nothing but foster distrust, rather than build the trust the relationship depends on. For those sales leaders or executives reading this book, just remember how much money it costs to earn a customer in the first place. Is this risk worth taking for a quick PO? We have to be more thoughtful than that, with so many competitors waiting for even a small crack within the relationship to open.

Relationship building as a seller is actually very easy. Just think about how you met your spouse, best friend, or new neighbor. No, I am not suggesting you treat a customer exactly as you would your spouse; we can all imagine the *Seinfeld*-like situations that would get us into. But do think about how you met your spouse or friends and the level of effort it took to maintain and grow that friendship over time. Focus your attention on that level of interaction as opposed to making them feel as though you are trying to sell something.

I spent my career as a seller and sales leader, yet I tell anyone I work with that I do not sell. I am a soft seller, meaning I speak with customers about their business and offer my knowledge on what my company can do to assist, but I almost never ask "Would you like to buy that from me?" or "Can I sell that to you?" More often than not, the customer ends up asking for my help based on the knowledge I share. That is a subtle difference, but it resonates strongly with me, my personality, and my style of selling. It is what makes me comfortable, and customers buy from sellers who look confident and appear comfortable. I share knowledge I have in the industry and look for ways they can improve their business, but rarely ask for the sale—yet I almost always get the sale.

Let me share how I handle relationship building by providing a few real experiences of customers I worked with in the New York area.

Customer Story 1: Go for the Green

I had been selling for well over a year to a Fortune 500 company that purchased staff augmentation and services from my company when its IT director scheduled a round of golf with me. (Imagine a seller playing golf with a customer? One of the perks of relationship building!) A few days prior to the round, the IT director called and asked if he could invite his boss, the VP of IT. Obviously, I said yes, excited to play a round with such a high-level executive.

But as we began to play, the VP seemed to be keeping his distance from me. He said hello and shook my hand, but beyond that he managed never to be next to me or make any small talk. I am a perceptive individual, and I could tell he was not interested in having a sales guy ask him a bunch of questions or pitching him a service while he was trying to relax. He did not know me or my style, so I fully understood the hesitation apparent in his body language.

The round ended, we all had a nice dinner, and we went on our way home to our families. Throughout it all, the VP said few words, and almost none were directed toward me besides a thank you for the golf and dinner.

Several months had passed, and once again I was scheduled to play golf with the IT director. Once again, he asked if he could invite his VP. I was not sure how the VP could possibly have had a good time the last round, working harder to avoid me than he did to hit the ball, but I agreed enthusiastically.

As I pulled into the parking lot that day, I was stunned to see the VP approach my car and say loudly, "Mike! How are you? It is very good to see you, my friend!" I won't lie; I tried to lean in closer to see if I could smell alcohol, but detected none. As we began the round, the VP shared a golf cart with me. The round was exponentially better than the previous one, full of good play and good conversation.

When the round ended, we went into the clubhouse to enjoy dinner. At one point during the dinner, the VP said, "You know, Mike, I get invited to a lot of golf outings and dinners. I hate going to them, because everyone always wants to sell me something. But you didn't. I really appreciated that."

From that day forward, the VP and I worked well together. I supported more of his business needs as years went on, and we enjoyed more golf together—all because, although I am a sales guy, I did not act like one.

The lesson? Do not sell during events. When a customer accepts your invitation, they are there on your dime, and they recognize that. You gain more from allowing them to enjoy themselves without the burden of the seller selling. Good things will follow.

Customer Story 2: Here Comes the Pitch

I was visiting our New York office and upon arrival was asked to attend a Mets baseball game with some customers as an executive sponsor. This is not exactly a stressful job requirement, especially since I love baseball, so I was happy to join.

Upon arrival to the luxury box the company had reserved, I was told this was a customer event where we would present some of our cloud service offerings and then watch the game. I was asked to be the presenter. I instructed the team to place their presentation in slide show mode and allow the presentation to run throughout the cocktail hour and game. Then I told them that neither I nor they were going to present anything. We would allow the customers who took the time to come to enjoy the game, food, and drinks. If they had any questions, they knew we were here.

Throughout the evening, multiple customer attendees made their way to me for discussions. These included questions about where I lived, my family, and my interest in baseball—as well as the customers proactively asking me to tell them about our offerings. I made sure to end every conversation with some version of, "I'm glad you joined us for the game. Hope you are having fun!" By utilizing implied selling, we gained new business with numerous attendees from the game over the next few weeks.

Attention, leadership: customers do not attend sporting events to see presentations. They attend for the sporting event, food, and drinks; they only tolerate the presentation. I am confident that you will gain greater depth in the relationship and greater potential for new business long term by focusing on their enjoyment of the event, rather than how fast you can read a bunch of slides to them.

Customer Story 3: The Night Before Christmas

I had a customer in downtown New York for whom my company provided maintenance and support services for Unix needs. I had a tradition of bringing the IT director out to lunch during the holidays. It was Christmas Eve, and I came to his office at 11:00 AM as scheduled. However, he was having a frustrating day: one of his applications had crashed, and he needed to get it back up and running before we went to lunch.

I offered to assist. My company was not skilled in that application, but it seemed like the right thing to do. Some time passed and his issue was not going away. He told me I could go, since he was not sure how long it would take, but I stayed to ensure he had his issue resolved. During that time, I made calls to others within my company, asking them to reach out to friends who might have the skills to assist.

Finally, I had lunch delivered to his office. As we ate, he called the company that developed the specialized software product that was down and causing a system outage, and was put on hold. As we waited to resolve this emergency issue, the theme song from Titanic began to blare out melodramatically over the speakerphone, filling the room.

The IT director raised his eyebrows over his sandwich and said flatly, "Can you believe this crap?" We burst out laughing, immediately diffusing the frustration.

The resolution finally came, and the systems were back up and running. The IT director looked at me and said, "You stayed with me all day, even though this had nothing to do with your business."

Although it was now 6:30 PM on Christmas Eve, it was easy for me to look at him and say, "I was not going to leave you alone. I wanted to help, even if buying lunch was all I could do." I wanted to make sure we got this taken care of together and show he could always count on me and my company, regardless of whether or not it benefitted us financially.

In all the stories above, relationships were what made for great business, not the act of selling. I didn't sell anything in any of these situations, yet at the same time I sold everything. Relationships are what make customers want to work with people they trust. Take note of my wording here: Customers want to work with people, not sellers. Stay focused on your customer every single day and make every interaction you have about them, not you.

> *Relationships were what made for great business, not the act of selling. I didn't sell anything ... yet at the same time I sold everything.*

I will close this chapter by discussing the value of communication, which solidifies the level of trust and respect a customer holds for the seller. In all my interactions with friends and family, both growing up and in business school, communication was considered a common courtesy and responsibility, and I feel the same needs to apply in my working life. Yet in sales, communication is often a lost art. The effort of maintaining consistent communication is easy for a seller when it is time to pick up a PO or when news is positive; I see few salespeople conflicted about making those calls. What customers struggle with the most (and what I struggle the most with as a sales leader) is why the communications stop if a sale is not pending or the customer is not happy. This reduces you back to that stigma of a seller who cares only about a PO, rather than a partner who has developed a tight bond of trust and respect. Trust, to a customer, means they can count on you as a person—through good times *and* bad.

What makes sellers, especially less experienced sellers, ignore customers if the buying process is on pause? We all have phone, email, and text communication available to us. In our modern world, we have no excuse for not maintaining a proper level of communication. If you have a car with hands-free capabilities, you can make a quick call to your customer while you're driving. A simple "How are you doing?" can go a long way to maintaining your success in that relationship. You do so with friends and family—add your customers to that list and take five important minutes to safeguard your future.

Along with the good, of course, comes the bad. Communication is never more important for a customer than when she or he is in need or experiencing a problem. Yet time and again, sellers go silent or try to avoid contact when those issues are related to the solutions they may have sold the customer. While I can appreciate from the seller perspective the need to want all the answers before speaking with the customer, that approach has more to do with what makes you as a seller feel better, not what makes the customer feel better. Remember: this is about the customer, not you. While you may not have every answer to every question, it is your responsibility to provide stability in that situation. Your ability to provide that customer information can be their lifeline for keeping their own job safe. Consider what the customer has at risk the next time you are afraid to speak with them, and try to provide some level of information—even if it is nothing more than assuring them that you will remain engaged until a solution is found. Will they appear frustrated every time you speak and the issue is not resolved? Perhaps. Will they value you even more after it is resolved if you maintained a proper level of communication with them along the way? Yes. This is easy—possibly uncomfortable at times, but easy nonetheless when you know that you are essentially holding the hand of a friend during a tough time.

As I said earlier, it costs a significant amount of time and effort to earn the right to have a relationship with a customer, especially when customers have many options available to them. Why put all the work that went into establishing that relationship at risk by going quiet after you have earned the relationship? Fear more the potential to lose the customer than the weight of keeping up proper communications, as these will buoy the customer during tough times.

Chapter 4

THE VALUE OF THE RIGHT FOCUS AND RIGHT QUALITY
Creating Outcomes from Consistency

I HAVE YET TO FIND A person to credit with this quote, but I'll note it here anyway: "Don't be the same, be better!" The idea fits quite well in sales—or should I say, it fits those who are successful in sales.

Here I want to highlight some guiding principles on which I have based my entire sales approach and apply across every chapter of this book. Their focus? Becoming better. In nearly every presentation I make to internal personnel or organizations, I describe my success model for sales based on the following key bullets:

1. **Customers first and foremost**
2. **Focus**
   a. Right customers, right opportunities, right solutions, right people (emphasis of this book)
3. **Quality, quality, quality**
   a. In our selling approach, our solutions, our planning

b. In every single customer interaction
4. **Be consistent across the business**
   a. In our messaging (internal and external)
   b. In how we approach all engagements
   c. In our preparation
5. **Win, succeed, and have fun**

I don't pretend that what I have defined within the bullets above is highly innovative, nor that it is something that others have not also promoted within their own businesses. I will, however, challenge the depth of many sales offices' commitment to applying focus and quality to everything they do within their business model approach and with daily rigor as I have for mine. For me, using these ideas as a guideline means that they have become our selling lifestyle in all the things we do. When we discuss prospective customers, we discuss how we earn that business by focusing on and applying quality in order to gain that relationship. When we discuss our proposal process, the discussion proceeds immediately to how we can ensure the highest level of quality in the proposed solution, focus our efforts to increase our ability to be successful, and expand discussions about delivering our service with quality. We do the same when speaking about our strategy and planning, leaders, people, pipeline development, and culture. This is a never-ending process of updating and adjusting our mindset, and it must include all aspects of the organization, not just sales, to ensure the highest level of customer intimacy and customer experience possible. If we do not work toward being the most successful salespeople and sales leaders we can be, we will not achieve the level of customer commitment we aspire to—the level that is imperative to earning long-term loyalty.

Customers First and Foremost

To sellers and sales leaders, customers directly represent the revenue and profit our company requires to grow our business. The customers are the life-blood of our business success, and as sellers and sales leaders, you are the individual who is responsible for creating a bond with them. This bond assures that their revenue and profit dollars are allocated to your company, not a competitor within the marketplace. Simply put, your job first and foremost in the eyes of your employer is to make your company revenue.

That said, my focus has always been on the customer, on finding any way I could to better understand their needs and how best to support those needs. A company I served as executive for many years, Dimension Data, embraced a valuable mindset that you as seller and sales leader should adopt early and live by closely. They used the following core employee value: "The customer is at the center of everything we do." The maxim was succinct and made it clear to all employees that the needs of the customer should always be at the forefront of our minds.

As a seller or sales leader, you have to value the benefit of earning a customer's business—and on a deeper and more important level, your relationship with them. While I do not detail the subject of relationships specifically throughout this book, every methodology or principle of my sales approach is designed to be leveraged with relationship selling. That is by far the most effective way for you to create and maintain a strong and lasting bond with your customers. This bond should be established based on honesty, transparency, and commitment to their success, not your own. Learn that and you will have the beginning of a long career in sales.

Focus

Relationships prosper when the other half of your relationship feels they are receiving your full attention. Customers may not always verbalize this, but when a seller hangs up quickly to grab another customer call or runs out of their office to visit the next customer, they experience a quiet feeling of dismissal. Of course this is not necessarily true in every case, but when it happens on a regular basis, they will notice the pattern in how you interact with them. Once a customer feels as though you are not giving them the attention you give other customers, they never forget it. Customers can be very quick to jokingly state, "Of course, I'm not your top customer!" Don't take that comment lightly. If it didn't have any meaning, they would not be saying it.

Focus in sales comes in several forms. When you speak with a customer, make them feel that you care most about them by providing them with your undivided attention. Ignoring incoming phone calls, emails, and text messages sends a powerful message that you are focused on them. Additionally—this is a big pet peeve of mine—when you are working on a response to a request for proposal, whether an RFI/RFP or some form of customer pricing request, focus your attention and your team's attention on that proposal only. If you truly feel your company is the "frontrunner," do not allow distractions to limit your ability to do the best job and provide the highest quality of response or submission possible. Create a standout personalized response, not a fill-in-the-blanks template designed to meet a timeline. Customers can tell when you have done nothing more than copy and paste other responses together; these responses lack attention to detail and leave them dissatisfied. It shows you either do not care about earning their business or do not know enough about it to provide them with additional information. Either way, they will not feel comfortable selecting you as a vendor if they cannot trust you or believe that you have applied a high level of effort and care. This is and always will be one of the best ways to assure you win business, earn trust, and retain respect from your customer with every work effort you support.

Quality, Quality, Quality

Consider how long it took you to earn the trust and respect of your customer and what a short time it takes to lose it. The difference often comes down to your ability to continually focus on applying quality to all aspects of your relationship. When the quality starts to diminish, the relationship soon follows—often at a rapid pace. There is a hard lesson to learn if you take your eye off this one important area.

You have the ability to prevent this from occurring. You just need to commit to your customer, all the people within your company, and yourself that you will never stop demanding quality in all aspects of your customer engagement. This is not as difficult a promise to live up to as it sounds, and it can be managed with a well-defined account plan and the willingness to put in the time. But it does take commitment. You must commit to demanding that your coworkers and partners respect how hard you work to provide your customers what you know they deserve: a great customer experience.

> **Never stop demanding quality in all aspects of your customer engagement.**

When you think back on your early interactions with the customer—when you first contacted them and throughout the initial process of wooing them (if you will)—you likely took extra time prior to every call and meeting to ensure that all your work was crisp, clear, and completely on point to the needs of the customer. In other words, you were applying your own level of quality control to your selling process. Now that they are a buying customer, can you still say that you apply a similar, if not higher, level of rigor to ensuring that all elements of your engagement are performed with that high level of quality? If not, why? Very likely you have become comfortable in the relationship; maybe you feel you have gained the extent of the customer spend. Most likely, you also have other customers to sell to and a manager who wants to have a growing pipeline with updates every other day. The pressure is definitely on, and it may cause you to overlook the small things you used to do. But the customer does not overlook it. You may not even realize that the customer is now giving some of their business to competitors.

Some of you may be thinking, "Not me! My relationship is strong—I always do right by my customer." If that's true, congratulations! However, I still recommend that you be open to assessing your relationship, if only to validate your assumptions.

Give yourself a gut check by honestly answering the following questions:

1. **Does the customer purchase the key products or services I offer only from me, or do they also do so from other competitors?**
2. **Am I sure that my company receives the majority of the customer's spend annually in all areas in which we specialize?**
3. **In the past 3-6 months, have I lost any bids or proposed business that I would have won in the past?**
4. **Has the customer expressed any level of dissatisfaction with our business or service?**

a. This is a tricky question. Some customers can be uncomfortable having that tough discussion, even with a vendor, so what may sound like a passing comment may be an indication of a disgruntled individual who is already embracing other vendors in discussions.

b. If they have expressed dissatisfaction, what have you done to (i) assist in the improvement, (ii) align the highest skilled personnel and/or resources in a timely manner, and (iii) remain involved until the resolution?

5. **Do you ask the customer for open feedback on a regular basis in an effort to improve your management of the account as well as how the rest of your company supports their business?**

6. **Do you ever ask the customer for their own definition of quality?** Don't feel bad if the answer is no; the reality is that most sellers and sales leaders assume that we and the customer are aligned on our definition of specific terms when in fact we never really check to be sure this is true. When both parties understand basic definitions differently, you risk leaving customer expectations unmet while you telling your own management that things are going great.

Spend your time wisely. Your company may have spent tens of thousands of dollars in resources and hundreds of man-hours to initially win that customer over. Don't risk losing a customer because you become too complacent to maintain or increase the level of quality control it took to win them over in the first place.

The key lesson here? Work always to balance your efforts across the many actions you need to take to assure customer satisfaction and differentiation.

Consistency

One of the more frustrating experiences a customer can have with a vendor or individual seller is inconsistency. This could mean a lack of consistency in the level of engagement, communications, messaging, delivery of the service, proposals or pricing models, personnel who support the delivery of the service, or more. As we've discussed, a lot goes into creating a customer relationship and even more into retaining the relationship—but there is no way as simple as just remaining consistent. And yet a lack of consistency seems to damage us all at one point in our sales career. Why is it so difficult to avoid such a simple mistake?

Some of it is due to carelessness. Some is to losing focus on what matters and not allowing longer relationships to make us complacent. Just as in our personal lives, there are many crossroads each day that can add to the perception that a company or seller's consistency is lacking. Almost all of these can be avoided.

Consider some basic issues that can drive a customer crazy:

- **A customer should trust a seller will call when they say they will call.** They rely on you and know you hold a cell phone in your hand. They also know how quickly you respond when an order is pending or a PO is waiting, and can see how that response differs when no PO is pending. Call or text when you commit to doing so.
- **Follow through on information when you said you would do so.** If you promise to send a proposal or information to the customer by 2:00 PM, but send it out sometime after 5:00 PM instead, you may feel that it was close enough, but the customer does not. All you have done consistently, from a customer perspective, is disappoint them. Keep in mind that they

may have promised someone within their business they would have the information earlier in the day; your tardiness makes them look bad in front of their peers. If something is delaying a proposal, the least you can do is keep the customer informed so they can do the same on their end to others they support.

- **A customer, especially a long-term customer, should feel confident that your pricing models are consistent, even if they have special pricing.** So why do we often hear customers complain that they have seen or heard of different pricing in different proposals for the same product? The seller has to provide some quality control on this, even if someone else is tasked with actually sending the proposal to the customer.

- **Ship dates, delivery dates, or service dates that are committed then changed or cancelled have a very negative effect on customer perception of your company.** Customers want commitments to be held by their vendors and hate to be disappointed—especially if they feel like the changes are due to our supporting a different customer first. This makes them feel less special. You live up to a committed tee time; live up to a customer promise. I do not disagree with the fact that sometimes issues arise that are beyond sellers' control; this is why it is critically important to do our work up front to schedule an event and properly validate a different checkpoint to ensure that nothing has changed. Throughout the process of waiting, provide the customer direct updates so they know the status and any risk that things might change at the last minute. It is always best to keep them informed throughout, regardless of the outcome.

- **Your company provides a service and you have defined measurements for success.** Let's say that a company has committed to answering 99% of the calls that come in to its support center within 5 rings; some months the company achieves this measurement, and others it does not. The customer view is that you lack consistency and they cannot rely on your service. Thus they begin to consider a more trusted vendor. I appreciate that as sellers you do not personally take the calls, but you do own the responsibility to work internally with your company to live up to things you promised the customer during your relationship-building process. Your own personal reputation is on the line, and you need to push your company to live up to the expectation that was agreed to.

Your ability to be consistent is a measure of the quality of service you provide, and customers take note when you do not meet those expectations regularly. My best recommendation is to remain close to the promises you made to your customer, inspect often, and remain committed to communicating with both your customer and internal employees as regularly as possible. Again, treat customers every day the way you treated them when initially creating the relationship, and never stop caring as much as you did when trying earn their business. We check and double check when trying to win the business and should never stop doing so due to complacency. Nothing is more important to keep, nor costlier to lose, than the customer you already have.

Tools and Analytics

Having the proper tools and analytics has tremendously affected my sales and sales leadership success. While I know this was not on my list earlier in this chapter, it is valuable to discuss, as it has everything to do with the rights I will discuss in the coming chapters. You need to know the importance of tools and analytics to your success and how best to leverage them to achieve the rights. Tools mean efficiency and productivity, which translates to improved decision-making and increased responsiveness to your customers.

A few tools I cannot live without are my CRM (SalesForce), Microsoft Office (especially Word, Excel, PowerPoint, and Visio), a good proposal generator, an RFP database search tool, a solid internet connection, and my cell phone. Having access to such websites as Gartner, Hoovers, Rain King, and the CEB Sales Leadership Council have also been a great help throughout my career. With such tools in hand, I am a more effective seller and sales leader.

I mention PowerPoint in my tools; I assume all sellers know how to use it to some capacity, and it can be very helpful. However, many sellers have forgotten how to use good old-fashioned eye contact as a communication tool. While it is perfectly acceptable to use PowerPoint to share a message or validate a point, when with customers I want to look them in the eye as long as I possibly can. Relationships built on trust are not strengthened because you can read content from a slide. Customers trust people who will sit across from them, look them in the eye, and deal with them in earnest. A PowerPoint is written information that can be shared, while eye contact creates an emotional bond and tells a story specifically about you as an individual. Customers have relationships and buy from individuals; make sure you are seen as a person, not a slide.

An additional tool that far too many companies overlook is a selling methodology. Examples are SPIN Selling or Miller Heiman. Both offer a much-needed selling process structure, and more importantly, some standards and consistency that can greatly improve a seller's ability to earn relationships, sustain positive business growth, and retain long-term customers. The methods these models utilize are proven successful and aid in creating the discipline and good selling principles that many sellers, sales leaders, and companies tend to lack.

Some may argue that these tools can fail, but in my view, this only occurs when the sellers, sales leaders and companies lack the discipline to remain committed to the models. I have deployed models and spent tens of thousands of dollars to train every employee—not just sellers—to ensure that all personnel who interact with a customer can follow best practices in the methodology chosen. Yet time seems to weaken their commitment, and once weakened, it slowly disappears overall. The tools make sense, but the discipline they impart will lose momentum if not strongly supported. That momentum is owned at the leadership level; it is the leaders who will dictate the longevity of the methodology, not the seller. Let's be honest: no seller wants to be forced into a methodology when they feel they have their own best practices for winning a sale. In reality, however, the methodology is not designed just for the seller; it is designed as an engagement model to best align all employees in the company, along with the customer and partners, for success. It is truly about the many and not the individual, which is why leaders must not allow the momentum to slow.

As a note, I do not personally recommend one of these methods over the other; both work well. The most important element for me is selecting the methodology that best aligns with your right strategy and right culture and that you commit to its use daily. Using it will only strengthen the skills and consistency of your teams, and like anything else in life, not using it will lead to losing it.

A brief comment on analytics before we conclude the chapter. I am an analytical person by nature; having the availability to review analytics greatly affects my decision-making process. Analytics is not the decision maker in this discussion—I am—but the analytics provide me with the clarity I need to inform my decisions. The best sources of good analytics are my finance or sales operations teams, who can provide almost any information I request for both pre- and post-sales outcomes. From a pre-sales or forecast perspective, all I usually need is SalesForce (SFDC) and Excel, which I can use to create my own worksheets for evaluating trends. Sales operations can provide any additional information on pre-sales level data, and finance is a great source of post-sales historical trends in customer purchases in almost any solution area of your business. When both are used in combination, you have limitless opportunities to make the quality decisions to run your business at the highest levels.

Chapter 5

THE RIGHT COMPANY MAKES A MAJOR DIFFERENCE
Make It a Match for Greatest Outcomes

"A man is known by the company he keeps."
- *Proverb*

YOUR PATH TO SUCCESS will largely be determined by the company you choose to work for and represent when developing customer relationships. This is true not just because of the reputation the company can provide, but because of all the other intangibles that lead to your ability to reach your highest potential. As skilled and talented as you may be, your skills must match the vision, strategy, capabilities, and expectations of the company you decide to represent to your customers. If they do not, think twice before accepting a role. In doing so, you accept the risk of experiencing challenges, frustrations, and unmet personal accomplishments. Do not take a job or role purely due to it sounding like it will pay more. Good sellers will always earn when the environment they select aligns with and complements their personal style. Far too many people fall prey to grass-is-always-greener thinking when money is on the table, but few experience benefits over time. Money is never the highest priority when choosing a company to work for. Best align the rights discussed within this book and your potential to earn will improve.

So many factors go into an individual sellers or sales leader's success, but the most important first step—after knowing *you*—will be synergy with the corporate environment you decide to embrace. This is not specifically about culture; I have a chapter dedicated to culture later within the book. This is about a company's vision, its strategic approach to business, its culture, its people, its base of customers, its capabilities and business offerings, its support structure, and more. When selecting your new company, be honest with yourself about the level of skill you possess and what brings that skill to the forefront and maximizes your ability to succeed. When you have identified that honestly and are confident that you recognize both strengths and weaknesses, you will be ready to find the right company. This right situation is one in which both you and the company reach the greatest potential for achieving higher goals long term together.

When the process of identifying the right company begins, you must consider yourself and the skills you possess a valuable commodity to whichever company you *choose to work for*. Listen again to the main words I stated in the last sentence: choose to work for. Of course, this may very well be the company at which you are currently employed. Identifying the right company is about looking for the best fit to accelerate your success, not simply doing a mass job search. The right company is one step to finding how to bring

> **❝ You must consider yourself and the skills you possess a valuable commodity to whichever company you choose to work for. ❞**

out the best in yourself. Be selective and find the company that most effectively maximizes your strengths and minimizes your weaknesses. You are the valuable asset in this scenario, as you have a skill the company needs.

We all look for new companies to work for at some time in our careers—sometimes by choice and other times by need. But how often, as you are considering your options, do you see yourself as the most valuable part of that discussion? Like most people, I felt butterflies as I sat for my first sales interviews, nervous because I felt a need to be offered the job even if I felt unsettled about whether I was right for the company. Later in my career, I was able to overcome this incorrect way of thinking. I shifted my attitude to one of confidence—and, to be frank, a "you need me more than I need you" attitude. This isn't because I am arrogant; arrogance has nothing to do with why I felt that way. I just realized, finally, that I am pretty damn good at what I do. Like many of you who have picked up this book, I have a high level of experience in creating sales outcomes, I work well with other sellers and the broader company base of employees, and I have the passion sales requires—so why not start believing the company gains a valuable asset when they hire me? While a seller certainly might need a company and their offerings to be able to sell and receive commission, the employer offerings do not sell themselves. You, as the seller, have that skill most required to turn products or services into revenue for the company. Feel confident that they need you.

That said, I also learned over time that if my skills are complementary to the manner in which the company does business and aligns well with the product and offerings they create, the likelihood of success is greatly increased for both parties. If I differ in philosophy, selling style, or if the company sells something other than a product or service I have previously sold, then the match likely will have less-than-favorable outcomes and leave both company and seller frustrated with one another. At minimum, my achievement will be limited in some capacity.

My recommendation for those trying to identify the right company to align with is to create a list of those things that are most important to you in a company and will benefit your style of selling or sales leadership most. Let me provide a sample list purely as a thought generator:

Does this company:

- **Have products and/or services that align well with my skills?**
- **Want me to support customers or a region that aligns well with my previous customer base and/or region?**
- **Have a culture that fits the way I like to interact and do business with my coworkers?** Think also about whether you prefer an office environment and face-to-face time with coworkers as opposed to a remote seller role.
- **Have supporting personnel with the technical skills to assist me in broader product or service discussions when speaking with customers?** If you need that skill to assist you, make sure it exists. If there are personnel with these skills, are they local and available to you and your customers, or will they need to be flown in? This may be meaningful depending on your product and style.
- **Share skilled resources across the entire team or give each employee their own?** How many people does a single skilled resource support?
- **Do proposal generation?** Do I do that myself?
- **Provide product training on a regular basis, or require self-training during onboarding?** If you are the type of

individual that needs more than just a pamphlet, check on what level of training is available.
- **Have a respected reputation within the customer and partner community?**
- **Have reference accounts?** If so, how many are within your region?

My desire was not to create the list for you, but to help you start to consider what matters most for you to recognize the success you desire with this company. Lists will differ greatly based on what is most relevant to the individual seller and sales leader. The primary objective is to recognize in advance the things that will most effectively lead to your success and trust your ability to find the right company that can match and support your capabilities, strengths, and goals.

As a sales leader and executive, let me share my number-one question for any company I consider working with as an employee or in a consultant capacity: "Will I have the ability to define my own strategic model for success? I am highly confident in my ability to create a model and hire people as I see necessary to achieve my objectives. Will I be limited in any way from developing and driving this type of plan?" For me, the answer to this question is the key to differentiating between potential employers. Will they allow me to control my destiny? Do they have confidence that when I assess the current environment and establish my own plan I can be successful? My belief in my own system is high, and if I deviate from my trusted methods I will diminish my returns. My insistence on using my own model does not in any way mean that I will refuse to align with the overarching corporate strategy, but my ability to craft my own business plan in accordance with that corporate strategy will make a significant difference for me as a leader. It is only then that I can align my skills to achieve the greatest level of success alongside the corporation-wide strategy.

Why does the right company matter so much—and why am I dedicating an entire chapter to the subject? Because not every good seller succeeds at every company. For good sellers to become great sellers, the company they choose to represent plays an important part. I have seen many highly skilled sellers leave a company where they were considered the most successful on the team to work for another company that made promises of higher earnings—then they languished. These situations occur when the new company is not aligned enough with the seller's interests and style to accelerate that seller's strengths and diminish their weaknesses. I have seen the opposite occur as well: a seller who has experienced only moderate success joins a new company, and suddenly everything just seems to click. Is it just luck, timing, skill, or the company enabling that success? It's all of the above and a lot more. Understanding that this can happen to you before it does is an important step toward your sustainable success. It is your responsibility to know what will bring out your best qualities, and you need to be vigilant when selecting the right company. Don't settle on just any company if you can avoid it.

Let me share some of the reasons successful sellers have given for failing at a previous company. The problems in the list are avoidable; it is fully in your control as a seller or sales leader to ask the right questions and pick the company that is the right match for you. Below I provide the reasons and my thoughts on each.

REASON 1:
"I did not get to sell to the same customers as I did at my previous company."

If this is a priority for you, it should be one of the first questions you ask in an interview. Consider the challenges that might occur if you do not have the same customers or are unable to acquire new customers in the same way. At your previous job, were your most successful customers handed over to you, or did you hunt for them and bring them into the company as net new customers? If they were handed to you to support and grow, starting with a new employer who expects you to hunt is likely to be a challenge. There can be a big difference between those who hunt for success and those who farm the land and grow better results. Know whether you're a hunter or a farmer and stick with similar roles.

There are a few other things to think about here. First, while sellers want to believe they are the reason the customer bought from their prior company and will follow them to the next company, be cautious. Most customers *do not* switch with you. Think about it: While few customers want to build a relationship with a new seller, far fewer want to go through the process of transitioning to a new vendor company and the many learning curves that occur along the way. Know for sure before you take a new role rather than assuming that your customers will change companies with you.

There is one other point to consider. If you asked this question in an interview and received an affirmative answer, did the hiring company truly commit that they would hand those same accounts to you, or was this a vague answer or an assumption by you? It is important to be clear on whether they will commit to every customer you ask for on day one or not. Sometimes you can have it written into your employment contract that those customers are yours to pursue for a certain number of years; do so if possible.

REASON 2:

"The technical resource was not in the region. I live on the West Coast, and the only support is located on the East Coast, so I had to wait weeks for assistance."

It can be hard to get a straight answer on this unless you ask again and again. I have heard of companies being asked, "Will I have resources available to go to customers with me?" and answering in the affirmative while knowing that the resources were located outside of that seller's primary geographic area. Unfortunately, you discover the more precise answer and location only after you join and experience it. I recommend more specific phrasing of this question during the interview process, such as, "My success in my current company has been a combination of both my own skills and my collaboration with my local resources on a daily basis. Will I have local resources available to me within my geographic coverage area? And if so, is it a shared resource, or will they focus on my needs only?" The value here is not only in specificity, but in being very clear that you are successful at your current company due in part to that teamwork. This should make both you and the interviewing company question how successful you would be if the resource did not exist.

REASON 3:

"I am used to selling products, yet this organization sells more solutions-based offerings. Not my strength."

This can be a challenge at best, and impossible at worst. I am not saying that people cannot make the transition, but many years of working with sellers in this situation have taught me that it is never a simple one. To even have a chance at making the transition successfully, you should remain within a company where you are already successful, experienced, and comfortable to reduce the learning curve process. Joining a new company is difficult enough; you certainly do not want to have to learn new offerings and entirely new selling processes as well.

While good sellers often convince themselves they can sell anything, transaction versus solution selling are not easily transferable for every seller. Be honest with yourself and never overestimate your skill. If you plan to call into the same customers, they will likely be more open to you adding new offerings to discussions if you remain with the same company. If you change employers and the product you sell, customers may doubt your level of expertise and thus question your trustworthiness as a seller. Customers do not want to be your test site. They cannot risk it.

REASON 4:
"They expected me to prospect for new customers. I'm a better farmer than hunter!"

This one is simple. Were they clear about the method of gaining customers in the interview? Or did they say something like, "You will receive some customers"? This leaves open room for guessing not only about how many, but about whether the customers you will get are established accounts that generate actual revenue today. This is another area where asking for full clarity is not inappropriate and is beneficial for both you and the company. It is your right as a candidate to know what the new company expects from you, as this can be a major factor in whether you succeed or fail.

REASON 5:
"Their compensation plan and quota were poorly designed."

Was it really poorly designed, or were you just unable to hit the number? It's a brutal question, but as I will say throughout this book, you have to be honest with yourself as a seller or sales leader if you expect to be successful. This is the complaint I hear most often. Missing a quota can be due to many factors, among them the four other points above, regardless of your level of effort and skill. Few people will not understand that, and I address it later in the book as well. But if you cannot find the proper momentum for success, face reality and figure out why so you do not ignore the need to make adjustments in future companies. Do not blame the quota if it was really on you.

I am going to take a moment to elaborate more on quota, especially since I hear this complaint even from sellers who are experienced and successful at their current company. My knowledge of quotas comes from the fact that I was not only a seller, sales leader, and sales executive, but I also developed and lead a sales operations practice for a $2B business; this included responsibility for compensation plans and quota creation efforts. My recommendation to top sellers or top sales leaders is this: If you plan to change companies, consider the quota ramifications. At your current company, has your achievement of quota been purely due to your superior selling or sales leadership skills? Or have you earned the right to a more favorable quota with a well-established list of customers because of your reputation for success among those you know? This is gut-check time: most of you know what it takes to get a softer quota, and you know when you are receiving one. Recognize honestly where this may have assisted your success, and recognize that if you change companies you must earn that level of respect all over again. If that is the case, you may be facing a challenging quota in addition to the possibility of the other issues detailed above. Do the math; if too many negatives appear, this is not the best change for you.

If we expand on this point related to compensation plans, we can and should know this information prior to accepting the role. During the interview process, ask to review the compensation plan prior to accepting the job or even ask to speak with current sellers or sales leaders. You may even want to learn about prior employees of that company by doing a search for all names that have employment history with that company on LinkedIn. You can send a message to former sellers and ask about the fairness of pay models and compensation plans. Sellers and sales leaders leave when there is a mismatch between them and the company that impedes their ability to learn and limit earning potential. Ask some basic questions to find out what those mismatches are before you make an incorrect choice for your future success. Another site to consider checking is Glassdoor, where current and past employees of a company can post anonymous reviews of the employer.

You ultimately know what feels right for you when it comes to compensation and financial expectations. Do the research to ensure that your new situation will benefit you.

Here is a quick list of things to ask about or research prior to accepting a role:

- **Base salary**
- **Variable pay structure (variable = commission)**
- **Quota-setting process**
- **A review of compensation plans:** This will allow you to see what exactly is written and if any elements exist that seem unsavory.

- **Speak with existing sellers:** Ask for their honest opinions. Don't just speak to the top earner on the team; talk with the lowest earner as well.
- **Compensation models:** Are these based on simple math (such as a percentage of every dollar sold)? Or are they based on a more complex matrix model? If every dollar sold has to meet a percentage of revenue along the x-axis and a percentage of profit along the y-axis, and your payout depends on some vague meeting point in the middle, ask for specifics. A former CEO, Jere Brown, who I highly respect as a leader, mentor and friend used to say that he wanted a compensation plan in which the seller could calculate his commission on the back of a cocktail napkin. Only you know which plan feels better, but know before you accept. My view is that complexity is intended to benefit the company, not the seller or sales leader. The company has the right to earn a profit and I accept that; I just want to ensure that you understand the model and know you can live with it before you accept the role and become frustrated down the road.
- **Overachievement:** Does this compensation plan allow for it? If so, at what percentage of payout?
- **Minimums and maximums:** Does this compensation plan have them? Do sellers only get paid when they surpass 30% of expected quota attainment, and does the plan have a cap on the high end? Both are important to know, especially if you have bills to pay and limitations on earnings could impact that decision. The 30% threshold means that unless your annual attainment is greater than 30% of your overall quota, the company will not pay you a commission. Regardless of the deals you close, you see no variable pay until you pass the

minimum threshold. I think it is crazy for a company to add caps to a seller's plan, but it does happen. Ask to see the plan so you can better review the details.

- **Be clear:** Interviewers want to entice you to accept the role, so they say a lot of things that sound good and might avoid clarifying the negative things unless you ask. Remember, they need your skills and you have the right to ask clarifying questions. Get the facts and leave nothing to chance. *Ask questions!* Any company that doesn't hire you because you asked too many questions is not the right company.
- **Factors:** For sales leaders, it is important to know how factors of your pay are determined. If you have a bonus plan, is it based only on your personal performance, or does it factor in a specific percentage on personal outcomes, a percentage on company-wide outcomes, a percentage on such things as employee survey results or performance reviews, etc.? Regardless of what factors exist, just know what they are and be comfortable in how you attain them.

Remember, these bullets are designed to help you ask enough questions to do your due diligence prior to accepting a role. They help avoid the risk of a disappointing surprise when you receive your first paycheck. They are not intended to make you critique or debate a company's plan as if they are cheating you. Companies have the right to be profitable, and they devise plans they feel appropriately contribute to their success, as do you.

I want to share another thought on compensation or pay structures related to selecting the right company. Beyond the pay models specific to sales personnel, it might be important to know how the company pays those in other roles, especially the roles that support you. Why? It may provide you with an indication of the level of skill your supporting resources will have. Companies that pay their resources at a lower pay scale than market averages may hire individuals who are relatively new or less experienced—not a good sign if you personally want to work with more senior-level resources. This will also indicate whether this company is going to have a retention problem in the marketplace and whether those with the best skills will be attracted away as their skill and reputation increases. It is thus an indicator of your long-term success of building sustainable customer relationships. Customers do not like when their vendor-related resources change on a regular basis. Ask questions on this, and notice the longevity of the employees on LinkedIn. It might help you determine whether this company has what it takes to match your skill with the success you desire.

One final consideration when choosing a company best for you might be the one we most often overlook as prospective employees. Ask questions in your interview or utilize tools like LinkedIn to see the background of the individual you will be reporting to directly, other sales leaders within the business, and the executive team. Why is this important? Their backgrounds may help you predict the future. More specifically, just because someone runs sales does not necessarily mean that they came from sales. If the person you will be directly reporting to does not themselves have a sales background, they are not likely to fully understand how best to manage you, make decisions in areas you deem important, and request needed changes. They certainly will not fully understand what to fight for and how to do so with passion. You have to know if that individual was given their role due to their tenure in the company, a gap in the company they were asked to fill, or because it was an area they wanted to try.

On a similar note, what is the tenure of the individual you will report to and the other sales leaders in the company? I worked with a company where the average tenure of the employees exceeded 15 years, and several key executives were in their roles for over 30 years. Over 30 years! This is not necessarily a bad thing, but in some instances it can imply that some people are more set in their ways and uncomfortable with the need for change within the business. If you are at an early or midway point in your career and benefit most when an environment allows for you to be creative, flexible, and sometimes disruptive, do not choose to work for a company where leaders are complacent and less willing to deviate from the standard approach they have embraced for years. Unless you yourself have full control and responsibility to make people changes in that type of environment, you may be headed down a frustrating path with an employer like this.

To close this chapter out, let me state again that you are the valued asset in this selection process. If the responses to your questions are not the ones you want to hear, consider wisely before making a move. Do not let frustration with your present company push your mind to ignore the obvious. Make the right choices to find the right company and move strategically.

Chapter 6

START WITH THE RIGHT STRATEGIC PLAN

Planning for the Highest Business Outcomes

THERE IS NO QUOTE that better sums up the success I have achieved in my career than that of Winston Churchill: "Failing to plan is planning to fail." Few quotations have been so succinct yet have applied so broadly to almost all the things we do in life. While he may have originally directed it toward the political realm, the need to plan for success is also seen throughout all aspects of business, sporting events, education, industry, and our personal lives. When is the last time you took a vacation with your family and did not plan out the transportation, lodging, and daily activities? Even on a trip to Disney World, you plan out when you will eat, go on rides, or take photos with the princesses. (Yes: been there, done that.) If you do not follow the plan as designed, you can experience unmet goals and your children will start to question your leadership abilities, resulting in frustration and unnecessary stress for all. So it goes with a sales team.

My one big regret is I had not learned earlier in my career the benefits, personal and professional, that could be gained from developing or following a properly defined strategic plan, whether as a seller or a sales leader. In my early days, I just picked some names from a directory and began dialing. I had no defined purpose other than to speak with someone and sell something; I had no defined model for what would make that call a success and no clear understanding of why my company would be a good fit for that individual, their company, or their business need. It was just a cold call, directed perhaps based on the person's industry or number of employees at most, and I was hoping to get lucky. It certainly had nothing to do with my own company business strategy and go-to-market (GTM) approach, or the customer's mission statement, as many work into their plans today. In many ways it was identifying one element I liked in the prospective customer's background, then applying the effort of relentless calls and dumb luck. As they say, even a blind squirrel finds a nut once in a while. When you make enough phone calls you eventually trip over a few nuts.

Thankfully I learned from those calls, absorbing the knowledge of what led to success and failure along the way. I began to consume more on business strategy and embrace input from others. I also began to work with more experienced leaders at different companies who demonstrated the use of strategic planning. I quickly realized that this not only worked better for me, but customers were more satisfied with my engagement, my sales results had improved dramatically and my quality of life had changed for the better. This was not only related to increased income (though that was nice as well); life was better because I worked more efficiently and found myself enjoying more free time with family rather than working well into the evening just to keep up.

I cannot tell you that the plan I discuss in this book will work for everyone consistently or the best plan for every seller or sales leader. Strategic planning is a matter of understanding how the process of defining a strategy looks and how to apply it with excellence with your business. I share some of my own experiences here, but you must learn how to be creative in your own business to gain the best results for you. The most important aspect of strategic planning is to first recognize the value of having one, and then crafting the right strategic plan for your individual needs and following that roadmap consistently.

What is strategic planning? The Balanced Scorecard website defines it this way:

> Strategic planning is an organizational management activity that is used to set priorities, focus energy and resources, strengthen operations, ensure that employees and other stakeholders are working toward common goals, establish agreement around intended outcomes/results, and assess and adjust the organization's direction in response to a changing environment. It is a disciplined effort that produces fundamental decisions and actions that shape and guide what an organization is, who it serves, what it does, and why it does it, with a focus on the future. Effective strategic planning articulates not only where an organization is going and the actions needed to make progress, but also how it will know if it is successful.

Is this definition the most accurate? To be honest, you can find thousands of iterations of the definition on the internet or in business books if you choose to look for one. All state the purpose in enough detail; I feel that the one above encapsulates the basic premise of what strategic planning is in a more consumable fashion than others, which seem to take an entire chapter to define.

Depending on who might be reading this book and your role within your organization, strategic planning is the most effective approach to your short- and long-term success. It does not need to be complex. Whether you are part of the leadership team that crafts the overall strategic plan for the business or an individual who plays a role in executing the strategic plan at the customer level, I urge you to take the time to understand what the plan means to you and your company and follow it in a highly committed way. It will prove to be well worth your time. I also highly recommend that if you are in a seller role, you spend the time upon reading your company-wide strategic plan and crafting your own individual objectives that properly align with your company expectations. This will help you articulate how you will best support the objectives of that plan with your defined list of accounts, target accounts, or regional responsibilities. Once you have it complete, share it with everyone within your business who contributes to your ability to accomplish those objectives you set for yourself, including executives as needed. That effort will pay dividends far more than not having a plan at all and hoping for the best. I promise that even for a seller, the use of a strategic plan will streamline your efforts, make you more efficient in your role, and dramatically improve your effectiveness and productivity.

Since there are already so many books written on strategic planning, I will not spend time rewriting the same materials all over again. What I will do is provide what I feel to be the most beneficial elements of a plan and how I have personally used them to generate success as a seller and sales leader. (One caveat: I am also quite analytical and have a background in building sales operations business units within organizations, so I will be veering off slightly into that world now and again in our discussion.)

The following seven bullets represent the core elements of a traditional strategic plan. The executive team will typically craft the vision, mission statement, and strategic master plan, along with some key goals and business objectives. In most companies the remaining elements are filtered down to the business unit owners such as the sales leaders.

1. **Vision:** Typically designed to be short and concise; meant to state what your company and its employees want to be recognized for within the marketplace
2. **Mission statement:** Why we exist as a company
3. **Strategies**
    a. Master plan: Typically defined to support the destiny of the company
        i. Tactical plan: Translates the master plan into specific goals or business unit responsibilities
        ii. Operational plan: Identifies specific procedures and actions required at lower levels within the company

    Note: *both tactical and operational plans support the master strategic plan*
4. **Goals:** What we must achieve for success
5. **Objectives:** Specific intentions expressed in measurable terms to achieve goals
6. **Activities:** Planned actions to achieve objectives
7. **Metrics and/or measurements:** Measures and indicators of success of activities

Since this book was designed for sellers and sales leaders, let's discuss what mattered to me when in those roles, which was the tactical or operational plan written specifically for my business unit or area of responsibility. This helped me leverage the strategic plan crafted for the overall company as the basis for my primary objectives, yet boiled these most important elements down to those I could specifically impact from my role. The seller and sales leaders have a responsibility to create tactical and/or operational plans for their business unit or individual area of responsibility only, which was ideal for me, as it allowed me to demonstrate support of the corporate strategy yet instill my own individual approach that best aligned to my strengths for growing my business.

That said, while the corporate vision, mission, and strategic master plans are set at the executive level, it is still of great importance that sellers and sales leaders deeply understand and align to each. As a representative of your organization, you will most certainly want to demonstrate internally your commitment to the success of the overall business. Your knowledge and alignment to the business expectations defined within the company-wide strategic plans will clearly illustrate this commitment. Additionally, your time will be heavily spent with external individuals such as partners, manufacturers, and customers who may themselves not know the plans your executives have developed for your organization, and your ability to articulate that message will be pivotal in their desire to work with you and your company. Never underestimate customers; while at times they may seem difficult to communicate with or show signs that lead you to believe they are not listening, they are. In fact, they are doing more than listening: they are often absorbing information that makes them either trust and respect you or quickly judge you as just another seller who thinks of them as nothing more than a commission payment.

Remember, customers want partners and vendors who will safeguard their jobs, help them make the best decisions, and know why vendor corporate beliefs align well with customer corporate beliefs. So even if you do not help write the vision, mission, or strategic master plans, your ability to share in those beliefs comes through in the discussions you have with customers, and this will assure them that you are a vendor who understands more than just a payday.

Vision and Mission Statement

Don't believe that you cannot have your own regional vision or mission statement that complements the overall corporate-wide vision and mission statements. There is nothing wrong with you having a more granular version specific to your team or customer base. I always do. Just ensure that it supports the overall corporate wide message and that it is concise. Below is a simple example of corporate and regional vision statements.

- **Company-wide vision:** To be recognized in the market as the premier service and solution provider through the continued growth of our portfolio of offerings and dedication to customer experience.
- **Regional or seller vision:** To be recognized in the Tri-State Area as the premier service provider for networking- and security-based technologies in the financial and pharmaceutical industries.

Take note of the subtle differences I highlight in the above examples. The corporate vision is slightly more broad, as they tend to be, but gives the customers the understanding that your company is a service and solutions provider and focuses on the customer as a core component to their success. It is short and concise, as it should be. Now note that the regional or seller vision still supports the corporate-wide vision, but allows you the ability to be slightly more specific to the customers you serve. The fact that the regional vision specifies the Tri-State Area, along with a focus on network and security to financial and pharmaceutical customers, more clearly demonstrates to leadership, customers, and partners where you plan to focus your efforts while also factoring in the broader corporate vision to support expanded needs.

Your company, customers, and partner community will appreciate your level of attention to detail specific to the area of the business most in your control.

Tactical Planning

Business unit responsibilities and their goals begin to most directly impact the seller and sales leaders as the plans created by the executive team are distributed down the organizational structure. This presents the first real opportunity for you to closely define the right tactical plans for your individual or team success.

The tactical approach you apply will define the responsibilities and goals you expect to implement and achieve the strategy you define. The tactical plan you develop should include a clearly defined yet measurable list of what needs to be done, how you plan to do it, the order in which the steps should be implemented, and any resources or tools needed for success. The tactical plan ensures that you and the others supporting your business understand what goals are important to your success. Some examples of goals you might set could include the following:

a. Win rate of 50%
b. Grow services revenue by 20% YOY
c. Be the #1 provider in my region for xx partner

Operational Planning

Operating plans are your ability to define the specific actions you plan to undertake in order to meet the goals you defined in the tactical plan. Recall that these actions are the individual steps to meet the goals that are created in order to align with the overall company business objectives. When I use the term "define," I mean keep it short and simple. I normally defined no more than three to five actions that would be meaningful to my outcomes but simple to administer and apply. Most people cannot keep track of more than three to five; the more you add, the more confusing is becomes and less likely to be considered effective. I typically used data points such as *sales will grow by x% YOY*. Few employees can challenge or incorrectly interpret your intentions when clear data within their realm of control is utilized. Allow the team and supporting resources to contribute their efforts to building this model.

Common objectives found within an operating plan are activities that must be delivered, expected outcomes for each objective, steps to monitor and inspect your progress, and defined resource requirements, to name a few. Again, for best success include the resources or personnel that will be needed to assist in the implementation. Their contributions to the development of the strategy will make them more likely to effectively implement and support your model. This is the most effective way to define how you plan to accomplish the actions you have developed for each day, week, and month. Some basic examples using one of the goals from the tactical plan samples we provided might be:

- **Goal:** Grow services revenue by 20% YOY
- **Actions:**
  » Retain my existing base business with focus on customer satisfaction in delivery while expanding existing customer spend by 10%
  » Identify and pursue 10 new service engagements with an average value of $xxx
  » Add new proactive monitoring service to every proposal

Obviously you will need to define your own actions specific to your individual business success, but this provides some basic guidance to help get you started. As important, if not more, than the creation of properly defined goals and actions will be the regular inspection you apply to assure they are being adhered to. I have used a high-level review on a monthly basis, just to validate progress, along with a more detailed inspection on a quarterly basis. While this may feel uncomfortable initially, as no seller or sales leader enjoys being inspected, I guarantee that as your success continues to improve you will feel the benefits of the effort you apply toward the inspection process.

Financial Planning

The strategic plans will have an overarching financial element to them, which is determined by the executive team. Most executive teams are quite open about the overall growth expectations of the company and why these need to be met. Some companies might communicate this information better than others, depending on size. Regardless, while it is a good idea for you to be informed and aware of the growth expectations of the business overall, the reality is that you will have a quota or budget that specifically shows your share of the financial responsibility for that fiscal year. If you focus on that, you are living up to your portion of the strategic plan related to financials (unless your leadership did a poor job aligning quotas and budgets to your strategic plan; while this is not always the case, I have dedicated an entire chapter to the potential challenges of quotas). You will also have the ability within your operational planning process to instill actions you specifically plan to undertake to meet those quota and budget expectations as discussed within the previous sections related to tactical and operations plans.

Sales operations business units own direct responsibility for the creation and development of regional sales budgets and seller quotas, so I have significant experience in this area. My immediate goal was always to fully understand the strategic goals of the overall business as well as the regional potential for sales. What does *potential* mean? Let me share the information I gathered, along with how I used it to create a financial model that was fair and equitable for all involved.

The information I gathered was simple:
- 3 years' revenue history for every customer who purchased something along with their primary salesperson
- 3-year buying history broken down by individual product, service and or solution along with their primary salesperson
- 3-year history for every sales leader and salesperson in the company, including revenue, gross profit, product, service, and solution they sold or lost
- 12 months of active pipeline for all levels of probability
- 3 years stack ranking history for each salesperson

- Understanding sales cycles or seller capabilities that could speed up or slow down the selling process and customer purchase patterns relative to average spend
- Any market-relevant data showing changes in the industries we served
- All information we had on hand related to prospective customers we were targeting
- As many customer visions and mission statements as we could capture, either from their websites or online tools such as Hoovers

In addition to the above, I named a team of people who were tasked with sharing ideas and input in the budget and quota creation process. This team included strategically selected sellers and sales leaders—some who were highly respected and fully understood the organization's strategic direction, and others who quite frankly just always had a reason to complain about their quotas. This allowed us to demonstrate to the broader sales community that we were soliciting feedback directly from their peers and gaining the value of their experience in the creation process. Let's face it: it also allowed us to demonstrate to the complainers that quotas were created with a team of their peers, thus disproving the persistent belief that "management" was pulling these numbers out of thin air without any rationale.

What I used the data to better understand were recognizable patterns. These were patterns in the existing customers' annual buying cycles, broken down in terms of how much they historically spent overall on products, services, or solutions. As a technology reseller, this could also indicate to me if the customer was due for a technology refresh or a project was set to conclude soon. I could also tell if the customer had expanded the number of product types they were purchasing from your company or if we still had an opportunity to expand the discussion with new offerings; this would become part of the actions for that new selling year. Just as important, it would indicate whether the customer was in good favor with our company and purchasing in greater volumes every year or cutting back on spending. Finally, we could tell if that customer was margin rich or if our selling efforts resulted in more revenue and less margin, which would potentially change how we sold to that customer and affect the manner in which quota was allocated based on either revenue, margin, or product type for the seller supporting that account. In other words, data gave us visibility and intelligence about how to make the right decisions for creating and selling the right strategic planning to grow our business.

Consider this analysis of customer data, and then imagine applying a similar methodology to assessing sellers and sales leader skills and their ability to support a defined quota or budget level. This was our next step. By "skills," I do not mean that we immediately graded salespeople as low performers if their numbers were low the previous year. On the contrary, skill in this case means that we can identify who amongst the sales team is stronger at selling product-based offerings, services-related capabilities, or our entire solution set. It also enables us to consider who has the most experience in sales and achieves more consistent performance outcomes. The goal was to ensure that through identification of customer and salesperson history, we could best match the right salesperson with the right customer and assign them the right quota or right budget to maximize their and the company's ability to succeed at achieving the right strategic planned goals. That's sounds like a lot of "rights"—but success is achieved when you align all the rights as best you can. The work it takes to build this process is both fun and immensely fulfilling when you achieve the success you expected.

This analysis not only made the allocation of quotas and budgets simpler, it took away the mystery for all the employees who had always wondered where the number came from. From the data analysis we had tangible information to demonstrate why the quota directly tied back to an assessment that most sellers and sales leaders had not fully known about their potential opportunity.

There is certainly a risk that this method will challenge the status quo; data rarely lies if analyzed accurately, and this can sometimes reveal inconsistencies or errors in the work we do. We now had patterns that clearly demonstrated that some sellers should be assigned to different customers based on sales strengths, which certainly caused contention. For some it was discouraging, as accounts they had supported for years were now being moved to someone else due to lack of growth, the inability to sell the necessary services to support the overall business strategy, or a need for change for some other reason. I am a strong believer that sellers are too frequently assigned to a specific customer for far too long, and that this can result in diminishing returns. While it is good for a seller to think *like* a customer, I caution that when salespeople can get so close to an account that they begin to think *for* the customer, believing they know what to discuss with the customer and what not to. This may have worked out fine for them in the past, since they make the same year over year commissions for maintaining the account and get to work with a customer who lets them call or show up whenever they want. (Easy work if you can get it.) Leaders

> **While it is good for a seller to think like a customer, I caution when salespeople begin to think for a customer.**

need to identify patterns in seller behavior or customer needs. Does the seller seem to decide the level of information shared with the customer, even related to new promotional items? Or do the financials show that the customer only purchases one category of product when in fact you know their business requires varied offerings?

A seller will seldom be supportive of an account change that takes away a long standing customer from their base of accounts but their sales leader must keep in mind decisions are about what is best for the customer and company. Rarely does the right decision for the customer not also improve the success of the individual seller as well. If we can tell the customer is not being supported in the best manner possible, change should occur, even if it feels uncomfortable to make that change. Yet time and time again, when I have made changes to this type of situation, the customer's spending pattern increases as both the new assigned seller and the customer explore new possibilities for innovative improvement of the customer's business environment never discussed by the prior sellers. We all win when it is done well.

A final nuance of proper quota allocation is that quotas cannot be determined by who the sales leaders like most, or who they decide are the best sellers (as opposed to those who truly *are* the best sellers). I have worked with numerous organizations in this regard and found consistently that the quota process favors those who are most connected to the leadership teams. While I understand how it can happen, facts are facts. Data has shown in countless examples that sellers who have the most experience and are deemed company best sellers are not always given the ability to prove that point by supporting the highest quota and best revenue achievement. Stack rankings are most often than not measured against attainment to quota, rather the year-over-year revenue growth or highest achievement of total revenue. If the person you've named your best seller is provided a quota that is easily reached just by selling their run rate of yearly revenue, they will essentially be at 100% achievement before the year even kicks off.

As sales leaders, you set the remainder of your sales team and your overall business success at risk when you do not align quotas with actual performance. If we hold those we believe are the best performers to lower standards and the least experienced to higher ones, we will receive a disproportionate average result across the team. That's right: As a sales leader, you already knew that. So why do these inequalities occur?

First, sales leaders are paid based on the combined success of the selling team, not by each seller's individual performance. This means that as a sales leader, you still make your goals even if the best seller does not get stretched to higher achievement goals or the least experienced falls short of their quota due to it being raised to compensate for the best seller's softer quota. Sales leaders also tend to justify that the best seller should be rewarded for being the best, which results in lower quota allocation and a greater opportunity to earn an annual president's club membership or trip measured against stack ranking outcomes. We are ensuring that those deemed our best people receive an easier path to go on stage and earn the extra benefits, while those who might have worked hardest and most likely earned the chance to be recognized are passed over.

This brings to mind a story from my past. A technology company I joined had an established team of sellers. I reported to the individual who was SVP of the entire East Coast region at the time—the same individual who used to run the business unit I had just taken responsibility for. I allocated quotas and the fiscal year progressed. Around midyear, I noticed when looking at the stack rankings that one of my sellers was in the top quadrant and aligned to be selected for the president's club if their performance continued. However, upon review of her YTD attainment to quota, the percentage of attainment did not appear possible based on the quota I had allocated earlier in the year. I came to find out that the SVP of sales had readjusted that seller quota by approximately 25% without conferring with me.

When I addressed the matter, he told me the seller had worked for him for years and had always been a top performer. He continued by stating that one of their motivating factors was the potential of being selected for the club and attending the trip, and it was important to keep the top performers happy.

I did not waver in my response: "You have over 100 sellers in this company. All of them want to make the club and go on the trip, and only 10 earn that right. You are handing it over to someone who has clearly demonstrated that they would not earn the right on their own. The data shows that the seller had generated increases in revenue every year, and you never raise their quota; in fact, you just lowered it well below their sales base."

The quota was changed back, and the seller was required to earn their way carrying the quota of a top performer. Now consider how many other sellers are given the same break in companies around the country; you'll begin to see why performance is not pushed to higher achievement levels. Much of the blame lies with middle management not expecting better from our designated top performers.

Let's close out this chapter by discussing the necessity of inspecting what we expect. While so many people in a selling capacity hate to be invited to a review session (unless it is specific to a best customer they can talk endlessly about), the value of inspection of our plans can be immeasurable. Properly applying oversight is important to keeping your teams properly focused on the right strategic plans for their individual and your company-wide success—and most importantly, their customer's success. Believe it or not, that comment has caused pushback against me in the past by the executive team. In some companies, the executive leadership does not see the world as I see—it in terms of putting the customer first and letting the rest fall into place. Some executive teams correct me: "You mean focus on the needs of the company first!" My response has and always will be the same: customer first. As far as I am concerned, if an executive team of your company does not understand or embrace that, it's not the right company.

Applying a high level of quality and focus to your inspection process will benefit you greatly. You are welcome to challenge my inspection theory by refusing to inspect—but by the time you realize what it is costing your business, you will be well on your way to closing out your fiscal year far below your quota and budget expectations. Save yourself now and do the inspections.

Here is a quick model for how I did inspections, whether my sellers and or their leaders complained or not:

1. **Weekly**
    a. Pipeline review
    b. Forecast
    c. Top 3 deal reviews
2. **Monthly**
    a. Quarterly projections
    b. Win plans for key deals
    c. Business plan review
        i. Mainly the monthly alignment to the objectives and goals (monthly is 2-3 initiatives only)
        ii. Review of next month initiatives
    d. 15 Minute account review (random calls to just validate status on primary deals)

3. **Quarterly**
    a. Business plan reviews
    b. Account plan reviews
    c. Win plans for key deals
    d. Customer-facing quarterly reviews (top 20 customers)
4. **Annually**
    a. Business plan reviews
    b. Account plan reviews
    c. Win plans for key deals
    d. New fiscal year plan adjustments/changes

The process may seem time-consuming, but beyond the initial round of inspection, the monthly reviews go quite fast. The ones that are designed to be more of a deep dive are the quarterly inspections. It is important, on a quarterly basis, to look more closely at the progress against the overall plan to see whether you are aligned or subtle tweaks are needed to ensure success. It is also very valuable during these reviews to include all the supporting team members who work with a specific customer or initiative. This validates their level of engagement but also allows the business owner to validate the commitment to the defined goals.

The old adage "inspect what you expect" is of great value to your success. It only takes a little time, but not overlooking the little things can earn your business millions.

Chapter 7

THE RIGHT MINDSET
You Can Achieve When You Believe

THEODORE ROOSEVELT ONCE SAID: "Believe you can and you're halfway there."

On a similar note, see Napoleon Hill's quote: "Whatever the mind of man can conceive and believe it can achieve."

I would never be one to profess that a strong belief system is *all* you need for success in sales. Without belief when selling, however, your journey toward success becomes a very steep mountain to climb. Belief can infuse your entire selling experience with a wealth of potential, both professionally and personally. Remember, sales can be a minefield of disappointment, especially as you are starting out. A strong mindset and high level of confidence will allow you to balance those emotions and persevere. My ability to have built confidence through my rights, combined with my passion for selling and sales leadership, enabled me to handle the challenges through whatever turbulence I experienced along the way.

In almost any office I reside in, I write the following on the whiteboard:
- **Think big…be big**
- **Think small…be small**
- **Only you can dictate your momentum**
    » A winning attitude leads to more winning
    » A losing attitude leads to more losing
    » Take control of your momentum

My primary point in stating that "you can achieve when you believe" goes back to my days as a telemarketer. I often say that you will never be able to sell anything, whether over the phone or in person, if the individual on the other side does not trust that you believe in what you are selling. Your tone of voice, your attitude, your body language, and your overall passion for your offerings can be heard through the phone or seen clearly across the table. Don't confuse passion with some sellers going into complete sales mode and being so high energy it just comes across as lying. There is a sense of calm that customers feel when they find that level of trust and respect for you as a seller or provider, and their ability to find that trust is influenced very heavily by the manner in which you handle yourself. You need to find the appropriate level of control and comfort in who you are and what you do and convey it properly.

Confident, not arrogant. Intelligent, not overbearing. Excited, not overdramatic. Your own sense of calm, which comes from knowing you have something special to offer that customer that can change the way they do business, is an attitude they can see and hear from the moment you say hello. Some of this is learned; you make an effort to consume information about your own business offerings, your awareness of the customer's business environment, and the ever-changing marketplace that can affect customers' buying decisions. This knowledge greatly impacts how you carry yourself with that customer. Almost anything can roll off your back because you know you are prepared and ready.

Having the right mentality and being focused on the right outcomes, and not allowing obstacles to deter you successfully accomplishing those outcomes, puts a lot of the right power in your hands to control. The very reason why having a strategy you believe in and company that best aligns to your capabilities significantly improves your success. Neither are a concern nor distraction to your best frame of mind when you make the right choice. Let me share with you an example of a sales results scenario that I have experienced across multiple companies I have assisted and that occurs more often than one would imagine.

During the 12-month fiscal year, a sales team has a team combined win rate below 20% and a loss rate just above 80%. Additionally, their wins resulted in an average win value of $51K, and their losses an average value of $157K. Neither result is desirable, obviously; indeed, situations like these are normally the reason I am hired to help improve the business. When I address this with the sellers and sales leaders, I typically receive a broad span of reasons; at least no one blames their dog for eating their homework.

What often stands out to me is not necessarily the specific excuses being given; many deflect the real truth anyway, in my view. What strikes me is the mood and attitude behind these excuses. For most, the tone often seems to be saying, loud and clear, one thing: "I give up." While they never actually state those words, if that is my perception as a leader, based on their tone and body language, would it not be reasonable to assume that customers sensed the same level of despair and lack of confidence? Let's face it: Who wants to buy something from a seller who sounds like they do not enjoy what they do or who they do it for? No customer of any product or service wants to hand their hard-earned money over to a seller who lacks the passion or confidence the customer wants to feel when they make that purchase.

What is stated openly is that nearly every seller and sales leader—the very ones tasked with selling offerings to customers—feels that, as a company, they cannot sell at the higher values or win more frequently. *As a company?* Does the company have the responsibility to sell, or do those who are now blaming the company for their own shortcomings? Self-awareness is a skill all sellers should be more capable or desirous of establishing within themselves; after all, we need it to reach the highest level of success. Being honest with ourselves can be difficult—and I do believe, deep down, that so many people are trying very hard to do the right thing and often extending beyond their true capabilities to do better. But this does bring us back to our discussion of right people in the right roles for the right outcomes.

The greatest detriment many of these sellers suffered from was their inability to believe that they could achieve at higher levels. That confidence to achieve higher. They had strong backgrounds in the industry and their learned skillsets about their offerings were actually quite good, yet their way of communicating with their customers did not dictate a proper approach to highest outcomes. They lacked the belief in themselves and what they were representing. This lack of belief can often be overcome with better understanding a person's area of concern or additional training and mentoring. Since I come from a technical background, when sellers and their sales leaders share this perceived attitude, I often pose the individuals a simple question: "Are you experienced salespeople, or were you just asked to take on that responsibility?"

That simple question can lead to Pandora's box being opened. The responses can open my eyes to the problem and include such feedback as a lack of experience, a lack of interest in the product or sales in general, and in some cases open statements that they had been placed in a role they never raised their hand for. This last input is not uncommon, especially in the technical realm, but can prove detrimental to employee and company. Technical personnel of varied levels of training who have been service technicians by skill, yet work so closely in a customer-facing capacity, can often be tasked with selling new offerings in addition to their technical responsibilities. They were neither skilled at selling nor even genuinely desirous to sell, but as companies work to get more out of every employee, this expectation can often occur. The best response I have heard from technical personnel has been: "I'm sick of being asked about why my pipeline is not growing. I have no idea how to do that." That one question can confirm the obvious, and I am often thankful we had had the discussion so early in the rebuilding process for each company. Now that the most visible obstacle to reaching success is identified, not having the right people in the right roles, it becomes time to change the mindsets the less than optimal decisions originated from.

The first stop is always those who wear the C on their chest. As I share with the executive teams and board members at these companies, the sellers and sales leaders tasked with the selling function are not bad employees; they had just been forced into the wrong situation, one that would not enable them to be passionate about what they did or to enjoy success along the way. They had not even applied to a selling role—they were just tasked with it and provided an informal version of sales training to get them going. This is a good example of how you get the outcomes based on the model you built and the people you assign to the task. You put people in the roles who do not believe they have the skill or capability to achieve at higher levels, and it results in more than 80% of the deals being lost and the value of the average loss being three to four times greater than that of the average win. The assigned sellers and sales leaders have not failed in this instance. The problem is that the leadership team did not truly commit to the right strategic plan and properly assign the right people to lead the charge. Heck, they were probably lucky that those sellers and sales leaders were able to win nearly 20% of the deals based on the situation and their true expertise.

The goal of this story is not to disparage a group of people. On the contrary—these companies where this has occurred were full of very committed and passionate people. However, they were incorrectly utilized, and were not assigned to roles that would more greatly foster their passion and overall confidence in what they were skilled to do on a daily basis. The story also provides a great example of how your ability to bear confidence in what you do plays a considerable role in the potential outcomes you are able to achieve.

Let me tell another story, this one about an infrastructure company I joined as their sales lead many years ago. Prior to my joining they had experienced what I will call stagnant sales success, and as a result, the sellers were feeling dejected. I'll add that by my own assessment, on an often-used sales skills grading-type scale, that group would on average have been a team of C sellers—there were no real A sellers at that time, and maybe at most a B seller. What made that slightly more challenging is that they themselves knew it.

Now, I will try my best not to cover the same story I cover in a later chapter—but let's just say we incurred multiple layers of transition throughout the business in hopes of increasing the odds and changing momentum. First we devised a right strategic plan for our region that all the sellers, sales leaders, and corporate executives felt confident in. We also shared selected portions of that plan with our strategic partners and customers where appropriate. We then reassigned accounts as necessary to better position the right people with the right customers in an effort to better align synergies and seller strengths. This would improve the very groundwork of what leads to great sales: confidence in the seller.

I decided, however, to take our plan one step further. We would consolidate it down to several small objectives to make it easier to feel our successes. Through reviews with various business units and customers, we decided that if we would give the team some basic goals, we could gain some level of positive momentum that could build team confidence. At that time, the company-wide win rate was 47%, yet the team I now led were 30-35% on average. Okay, so I would focus there first.

You will find that win rate is always a primary focus area for me as a leader; if I were to be held to a single goal for my business, it would almost always be a focus on win rate improvement. This is because it is the single easiest measurement to monitor and influence, and it also presents us with the simplest way to increase momentum and positive energy within the business. Win rate tells us many things about the business and those who work within it. Another reason to focus on win rate is that once you have accomplished the benefit of achieving a higher win rate, which leads to increased revenue attainment, you can expand on the win rate goal by challenging your team with also increasing the average size of the revenue per sale. This accomplishes two important criteria: increasing the win rate from 35% to, say, 50%, while also increasing the average size of a sale from being, perhaps, $51K to $75K. Both change business outcomes dramatically, and beginning with just win rate alone allows for a subtle transition to the other as the sales leader begins to recognize improvement.

TABLE 2: BEFORE

	BEFORE					Calls
	MONDAY	TUESDAY	WEDNESDAY	THURSDAY	FRIDAY	Lunch
8:00 AM	Calls	Calls	Calls	Calls	Calls	Emails
8:30 AM			Partner Call		Partner Call	Proposals
9:00 AM	Prep Work	Client 4 Preso	Prep Work	Partner Meeting	Prep Work	Partners
9:30 AM						Prep Work
10:00 AM	Weekly Forecast	Partner Call	RFP Response Call	RFP Response Call	Client 12 Meeting	Client 1
10:30 AM		Prospecting				Client 2
11:00 AM	Client 1	Client 5 Call			Client 13 Meeting	Client 3
11:30 AM						Client 4
12:00 AM	Lunch	Lunch and Emails	Lunch and Emails	Client 9 Lunch	Lunch	Client 5
12:30 AM						Client 6
1:00 PM	Partner Call	Calls	Client 7 Call	Calls in Car	RFP Response Call	Client 7
1:30 PM	Calls in Car		Calls in Car			Client 8
2:00 PM	Client 2	RFP Response Call	Partner Call	Client 10 Meeting		Client 9
2:30 PM			Calls in Car			Client 10
3:00 PM	Calls in Car		Client 8		Calls	Client 11
3:30 PM	Proposal	Client 6 Call		Calls in Car		Client 12
4:00 PM	Partner Call					Client 13
4:30 PM	Client 3	RFP Response Call	Proposal and Emails	Emails	Proposals and Emails	Client 14
5:00 PM						Client 15
5:30 PM	Emails			Calls in Car	Calls in Car	Client 16
6:00 PM						Client 17
6:30 PM	Family Time	Family Time	Family Time but also dealing with client issues	Client 11 Dinner	Family Time	Client 18
7:00 PM						Client 19
7:30 PM						Client 20
8:00 PM	Prep Work for Preso	Proposal and Emails				Client 21
8:30 PM				Proposal		Client 22
9:00 PM						Client 23
9:30 PM						Client 24
10:00 PM						Client 25

To show some level of improvement and build confidence quickly, I told the sellers I didn't care what they sold—just sell it and increase that win ratio, with an initial goal of 50%. The 50% did not seem unattainable based on where the team was already, and I could see by inspecting past win/loss reports that it was easily achievable with just a few small changes to our current approach such as less focus on low probability opportunities. It was neither a lofty goal nor one that disrupted the sellers' current approach to selling, but it was one that could change their mindset of being successful in a short time frame.[1]

In addition to win rate, I told them, for the next month focus as much of your attention as possible on each of your top five accounts. This will ensure that our efforts are within the customers that know us and a sale can move through the selling process quickly. Finally, there would be a new goal would be that no sale be closed with more than three proposal revisions moving forward. The average at that time was six revisions prior to closing, and the proposal team was getting agitated. The sellers' normal practice was to bring a proposal with them to an initial meeting before they ever knew the needs of the customer; this was a shot in the dark that could be prevented with increased needs awareness efforts from the outset. Having a goal to limit the number of revisions required the sellers to spend more quality time with the customer, asking important questions and discussing their business issues, rather than just randomly handing them a proposal that made little sense and did not demonstrate any level of knowledge of the customer environment. These were small nuances that the customers most likely found irritating and hindered the sellers truly building a strong relationship.

Small goals paid off. The sellers began to win. Additionally, because we focused on our best existing accounts and reducing revisions to proposals, customers became more comfortable that the sellers understood their business needs, and the sales cycle actually

---

[1] I realize that this contradicts what I write in this book related to the right solution. In this case, however, it was more important to build confidence first and focus on right solution once confidence was where it needed to be.

shortened. Within the year we had improved from the 30-35% range to the highest win ratio across the company—over 60%. The other benefit was an increase in employee satisfaction specific to the proposal team. With the significant reduction in the number of revisions that team had experienced, they were able to spend more time developing proposals of higher quality. They felt that they had finally reduced what they considered busywork and were spending time on quality work that led to more wins. In addition to increasing their satisfaction, it greatly improved the relationship they had with the sellers, as now they were beginning to enjoy the benefits of collaboratively winning more often. The office environment improved as a whole, as fewer arguments arose, and the customers enjoyed richer and more innovative proposals, smoother interactions with both teams, and less confusion and distrust.

That story can fall under the chapters related to right culture, right people, or even right solutions as easily as it could in this section, but I share it here because it illustrates how when you focus on doing your work with the right quality, it can begin to change your mindset and create more positive results.

That quality did require some changes in selling approach for sellers and others at the company. As I noted in Chapter 4, I am a strong believer in focus and quality for driving success blended with a firm commitment to the customer's needs first. You get those right and your success will grow so rapidly it may feel overwhelming. A winning attitude leads to more winning; and when part of the team experiences initial winnings, others on the team and across the business begin to feed off that energy and want to experience it themselves. The real challenge is finding the right place to focus on: Where do we look to increase the win rate from 40% to 50% or otherwise gain enough momentum so the entire team can feel that winning attitude?

I mentioned earlier that when I first joined one infrastructure company, I needed the team to align with my methodology and logic related to customers. Gaining this commitment from an entire team when you are the "new guy" is never simple, so I knew I needed a way to test my approach and show others how it worked in a successful way. I spent that first three months in the company not only learning about the business and customers, but also about my team members in order to understand how I could help each. The time was right to select the individual I felt could propel my methodology to success.

One day I asked one of the sellers, James, to join me in my office and to bring his customer list. In this region the sellers had an active customer base of approximately 320 customers spread across 5 sellers—in other words, around 60 active customers per individual seller to support, maintain, and sell. That ratio did not match my approach to sales effectiveness at all; I needed to gain an ally if my selling methodology were to gain any positive momentum in this environment.

James was well known across the region team, the company, and the partner community, but stood out as someone who even though he had been achieving success was struggling with the workload balance of his customers, his partners, and his personal life. He always seemed to be overworked, but his work lacked the level of quality a winning seller exhibits. As a result, partners were becoming upset with his inability to engage with their shared customers in a meaningful way. Customers had provided similar feedback, often stating that his presentations and engagement with them seemed to lack proper preparation. Around the same time, James had also lost a large deal ($2M). A customer had weeks earlier given him a verbal commitment to purchase, but ultimately he lost the deal when he did not remain engaged and a competitor found a way in and stole it from under his nose. He seemed the ideal individual on whom to apply my selling methods. I knew he had the mindset to excel.

As he entered my office, James could see that I was primed and ready to use my large whiteboard for the discussion. The whiteboard was newly cleaned (I am quite anal about whiteboards). I had drawn a weekly schedule covering Monday through Friday across the top; down the left were the hours from 8:00 AM to 11:00 PM. Nothing was written on the inside. After a brief discussion, I asked James to write all his customers' names to the right of the blank schedule. This was an important part of the exercise, as it visually demonstrated how many customers he worked with. Once written, he and I stood next to the board and discussed how he plans out his week and how that would lead to his achieving success. Keep in mind that many things could occur in a week, including emails, phone calls, drive time to appointments, proposal responses, RFP responses, customer meetings, and partner meetings, as well as of course lunch and family time later in the evening. Everything I just mentioned was also written on the board so that we could see visually what needed to be done in a given work week.

Now that the board was ready I asked James to enter his number one customer into the schedule, but to only take up the amount of time he believes he spends each week on building a strong relationship with that customer. If he only saw a customer every other week for, say, two hours, he should add them into the weekly schedule as a one-hour weekly occurrence. The point was to account for the time per week he had to work and think about the actions he took. We did the same for his second-best customer, third-best customer and so on, then began to enter how much time he spent conducting phone calls, responding to emails, and calling partners. The board began to take shape and the times of the day were filling up fast. When he was done the schedule looked not unlike Table 2, but much messier—filled with whiteboard eraser marks, strikethroughs, and numerous attempts to overlap time and multitask. Focus and quality do not align with multitasking; I instructed him to focus on one customer or task at a time and do it with quality. Only when it was done well should he move to the next item.

What I needed him to see immediately within the schedule was whether he was using his time management to his advantage and who was benefiting from how he managed his day. Specifically, I was trying to see if he recognized that in doing what he defined as being "necessary" to manage his customers properly, he was only able to enter a total of thirteen customers into his schedule (those highlighted in blue), not the 60 assigned to him. What is not clearly reflected is how he dealt with the customers that were not written onto the schedule; they all fell into the email or phone call category. In other words, he was giving them little priority—only enough attention for him to believe he had done his job.

That is what is called "kidding yourself" in sales and a vast majority of us do it. He had also neglected to enter one important part of the day onto his schedule: lunch. I was trying to get him to see that he was not applying focus and quality to his work efforts, but just trying to get it done and make everyone happy. In sales, when you try to make everyone happy you make no one happy. So focus on what matters and have the right strategic plan to start with.

We discussed the schedule for quite some time, and he opened up about how hard it was to keep up with everything. He was frequently running behind, often trying to create the presentations he planned to

> **When you try to make everyone happy you make no one happy. So focus on what matters.**

present to customers in the morning right before he went to bed the night prior. This led not only to him lacking focus on the task at hand, but also to him being too tired to apply the proper level of quality. It also caused his family frustration, as he never focused on them when he was home. I shared with him my selling approach and told him that I believe less is more when it comes to customers. We would focus on fewer primary customers and apply a higher level of quality, and due to the increased relationship, broader engagement, and deeper knowledge of their business, we would receive more growth in revenue while also reducing the chaos in his day. As simple as that.

I tasked right then and there will identifying the eight customers he felt were his best and could prosper the most from him focusing his time and efforts only on them. The rest would go back into the office pool or to an inside model I was defining. We discussed the benefits of a true quality customer relationship and what it would mean for him both personally and professionally, not to mention the benefit to the customers and partners he supported. His face was pale, and I could sense his trepidation over the reduced base, but to his credit committed to the model and to a new schedule looked similar to Table 3.

TABLE 3: AFTER

	AFTER					
	MONDAY	TUESDAY	WEDNESDAY	THURSDAY	FRIDAY	
8:00 AM	Calls	Calls	Calls	Calls	Calls	Calls
8:30 AM						Calls
9:00 AM	Prep Work	Client 4 Preso	Proposal Response	Partner Meeting	Client 8 Meeting	Lunch
9:30 AM						Emails
10:00 AM	Weekly Forecast		RFP Response Call	RFP Response Call	Office time to work with support	Proposals
10:30 AM						Partners
11:00 AM	Client 1	Partner Meeting				Prepwork
11:30 AM						Client 1
12:00 AM	Lunch	Lunch	Lunch	Lunch	Lunch	Client 2
12:30 AM						Client 3
1:00 PM	Partner Call	Calls	Partner Call	Client 6 Meeting	RFP Response Call	Client 4
1:30 PM						Client 5
2:00 PM	Client 1	RFP Response Call	Client 5	Calls in Car		Client 6
2:30 PM						Client 7
3:00 PM	Calls in Car				Calls	Client 8
3:30 PM	Proposal Response	Client 4 Call	Meet with Manager	Client 7 Meeting		
4:00 PM					Proposals and Emails	
4:30 PM	Client 2					
5:00 PM		RFP Response Call	Proposal and Emails	Proposal and Emails		
5:30 PM	Emails					
6:00 PM						
6:30 PM						
7:00 PM						
7:30 PM						
8:00 PM						
8:30 PM						
9:00 PM						
9:30 PM						
10:00 PM						

The new schedule was much simpler for him to manage. What I had to prove, however, was that simplicity would also lead to greater success; essentially, less is more. James now had freed himself of the burden of spending countless hours making phone calls and responding to emails from customers from his original schedule. Instead he took what amounted to 10-15 hours a week and refocused his attention on only those eight customers he was looking to expand his relationships with. Now the meetings he even had with an individual customer or partner were no longer restricted to an hour; his average time increased as they became his priority, and he had the opportunity to meet more people within each. A final tweak we made to the model was to align James with the same partner rep on every account. They had good rapport together, and I saw nothing but positives from allowing this one-for-one alignment.

The plan worked. Though James was nervous initially, he embraced the change with confidence and a new level of energy. His customers and his partners noticed the change; his entire demeanor became incredibly relaxed and focused, and the quality of his work increased significantly. About six months later I attended a quarterly business review with his top customer, the largest energy company in the state, and the primary partner rep. Upon seeing me the customer was quick to say: "I have to tell you that between James and the partner rep, this is the best vendor relationship we have ever had. It has been a pleasure working with your company." This was validation not only for the plan, but also for James to know his commitment to the approach was showing the results we discussed it should.

Within the year James, his customers, and his growth in revenue were flourishing—so much that during the next fiscal year annual kickoff meeting, James was announced as a top performer and earned the right to attend the president's club for his efforts. This was made more impressive by the fact that company's president's club was only for the top ten earners across the entire country; James was in North Carolina, not New York or Chicago, so people took notice.

This led to the next, and most important, step. The other sellers on the team were now coming to me to ask how they could get similar results. The schedule went back up on the whiteboard four more times. The right strategy was beginning to gain momentum, and it was due to our ability to demonstrate success early.

Good sellers all want to be successful at their jobs, and when the good ones see success they are happy to try and replicate it. Being a copycat in sales is actually a winning strategy, not something that's frowned upon. Sellers by nature fear the risks associated with being the first to try anything, especially since when something unproven goes wrong a seller could lose a customer's business and their commission. The sellers now had the right mindset to commit to the right strategy, which was critical to region-wide success. I credit James for taking that risk and placing trust in someone he barely knew and a methodology that could have gone completely wrong had he not committed as he had. His confidence in the methods, commitment to following the plan, and the passion he demonstrated in his success says a great deal about why it worked for him.

Let's fast forward and finish the story. The right mindset was now established within the region, with the right strategy, the right people, the right leadership, and right customers ready to go full speed. We were ready with our rights in place, and results began showing that it was working. That year we were able to achieve 125% of quota as a region, the win rate was steady above 60%, and customers began requesting more time from us to discuss their needs. Just as important, our small region was having fun, winning deals, and spending more time than ever strategizing as a team in ways to expand the customer relationship. The mindsets of the 45 people in the region had begun to run in unison, locked in on success.

I led that business as a GM for three years. In that time the team tripled its business revenue, maintained a win rate of 60-65% for the region, and were able to take home more company awards at the annual kickoff each year than any other region. We also saw two sellers within our small region take two of the ten president's club slots consistently. I knew the results were possible all along, but I could not have been more proud of the team. They all believed so deeply in their desire to be successful that they fully embraced the necessary steps we created to pursue our rights, and their commitment paid off for them. Taking a risk is brave, but being committed to an area of uncertainty and trusting it will work out for your career illustrates an extraordinary strength of character.

The right people with the right mindset changed their world.

Chapter 8

THE RIGHT LEADERSHIP TO MAXIMIZE YOUR OUTCOMES

The Value of Leadership that Leads from the Front

IN THE BOOK *GOOD TO GREAT*, Jim Collins makes an invaluable point when he talks about "getting the right people on the bus, the wrong people off the bus, and the right people in the right seats." He writes:

> The best executives have always focused first on getting people who share their values and standards. They understood that vision and strategy cannot compensate for having the wrong people. Once you have the right folks in place, it's much easier to steer the bus as conditions change.

I could not agree more. This is especially true when it comes to leadership roles, as leaders are responsible for hiring personnel throughout the organizational structure, training all new hires on aligned values, standards, and business expectations, and ultimately driving sales outcomes. If any individual leader does not properly support the corporate vision with their actions and words, all employees managed by that individual will also be at risk of not properly supporting the vision, leading to diminished outcomes. In doing so, over time the business and the people within will most assuredly fall short of its truest potential.

Much to Collins' point, getting the right people on the bus and the wrong people off will make a world of difference to your business success. However, more often than not sales executives make decisions using the outcomes of the field-level sellers as benchmarks of success or failure. In other words, they look at the stack rankings to see who succeeded and who failed, and perceive employees with lower numbers as "at-risk employees." My contention with this thinking is and has always been that middle managers, the sales leaders, play a more important role than do the actual sellers in sales outcomes. The sales leaders build regional strategic plans to support the company-wide plans, they build compensation models to support those plans, they hire, onboard, and train the sellers, and they define the primary initiatives and actions to be taken—yet if sales fall short, we blame the sellers? Sellers only sell what and how they are told to sell based on the defined strategy and direction from sales leaders. That is the only responsibility most sellers are given in this model, yet when it fails they bear the brunt of the blame. As we head deeper into this chapter, I urge the sales community to stop thinking as we always have and begin to view this more holistically if we all expect to achieve improved outcomes.

Albert Einstein stated: "We can't solve a problem using the same thinking that created it." I like this quote, as it goes directly to the heart of the problem many companies experience in maximizing their growth potential. Don't fool yourself into believing that the leaders you have been on board for a number of years are doing a good job because they attained 101% of their budget last year. Look more closely: Did they actually miss out on attaining 150% of their budget when that level of success was possible? Are they really the best leaders for the direction in which our business is headed? Did only four of our eight sellers reach 100% attainment because four sellers are inferior, or was the regional modeling incorrectly defined to reach maximum potential? All too often we rationalize that our existing sales leaders, directors, and VPs are making progress, and that if problems exist, they lie more in the field sellers' failures to close rather than the actual leaders at the helm. While field sellers may be falling short of expectations, they do not work autonomously and without direction from someone. Why is it so difficult to acknowledge that the field seller may be failing due to incorrectly set expectations or poor management? The sales leaders are responsible for hiring field sellers, defining their goals, managing their objectives, and setting quotas, among other things; yet when the sales leader tells the executive team a field seller is underperforming, it is rarely questioned whether they are being poorly managed.

Let me share another sales results scenario that I see all too frequently in technical based sales and it relates to preventing lost opportunities. Many tend to find fault in the seller when a loss occurs; while sellers certainly have their faults, I feel the leadership also bears accountability in these scenarios.

Employee Story 4: Pride over Outcome

Your best sellers are uncovering new opportunities across their many contacts within a customer. In doing so, a seller learns that a customer has been planning to outsource a large portion of their IT services. This is great news for the seller, as they have been waiting for a significant opportunity to come along. For them, this has the potential to broaden their relationship with the customer but also expand their earning potential. The excitement is high!

Upon receipt of this new opportunity, the seller moves quickly to qualify the opportunity and gain executive-level approval to pursue what could be a large opportunity. Executives can often be excited about the potential a large engagement brings to achieving their yearly budget so gaining their commitment can be easy especially if they trust the seller. Sounds good right? Well, a closer look is needed since this can be the beginning of a tough process.

The primary challenge often encountered is the lack of positioning the company has to win many of these more complex engagements. Remember, the seller just happened to come across this opportunity. They had not known well in advance of the opportunity nor did the customer solicit their insight as a trusted advisor. In other words, they are not perceived by the customer as an industry expert for this need. The second challenge these engagements can face is the desire by the seller to be in control of the response process. Even though they have little to no background in this very specialized area of the business their confidence and need to be in charge stands front and center. With many technical responses especially outsourcing, the seller has neither the experience or technical skill required to respond to the request nor the proper level of capabilities this complex an offering requires to manage the effort. The most effective way for a seller to assist is to hand the opportunity off to the personnel within the business who had deeper understanding of the requirements and years of experience in supporting such needs. Yet, from experience, I can tell you that the sellers often do not allow the true experts to manage the process, which includes managing the customer relationship, and often gain executive support to run the initiative themselves.

Let's fast forward. The response is complete and submitted to the customer for review. Let me look back on what likely occurred during the response process so I can share where a traditional seller fails to foresee the benefits specialized teams offer this level of response. What is most important to understand first is "can we win?" Why is that the first question? A seller looking for a commission is quick to overlook the obvious. Leaders need to be asking better questions before a pursuit: "Are we well positioned to win?" What does this mean? Is our customer relationship such that we are considered their primary consideration, are we the incumbent provider today, do we have the skills and capabilities in place today to be successful at delivering the service, will we have the ability to provide the customer the value they are looking to receive, who within the customer will be our advocate, and more.

In more of these scenarios than I am happy to share, I will tell you that the responses result in lost opportunities. Why? Many of the reasons stated in the last paragraph play a role. Some opportunities simply should not have been responded to at all, yet the qualification process overlooked basic disqualifiers. All too often, the sellers' lack of expertise but demand to own the process impeded their ability to be effective. Recall that I mentioned earlier in the book it is OK for sellers to think like a customer but should never think for a customer. That comes into play especially when technical personnel want to ask the customers clarifying questions and sellers do not want to bother the customer or fear they will look like they lack knowledge by asking too many questions. Sellers can often overlook important elements of a complex response by minimizing their importance, yet the technical team knows differently from their experience in this space.

In the end a significant amount of money was spent on the pursuit of the engagement, yet the response was not provided the highest level of quality both from a standpoint of input and skilled personnel to respond. The customer now is concerned about you as a provider as your response has left them wondering if you truly are the right company for their broader business needs.

The scenario I am using is real and not unlike what occurs every day in companies across the country. For me, this is not only unfortunate but incredibly careless and shameful from multiple standpoints—especially for someone like me, a career seller with a passion for and focus on quality. I consider all parties in this example at fault to some degree. The seller allowed pride and ego to stand in the way of their potential for success, and the leadership and executives, who at any time during the engagement could have made a different leadership decision, yet chose to support it. Strong leadership would have recognized the value of the expertise they hired to assist the company with just this type of situation. Leaders must make decisions that suit the best interests of the business without concerning themselves with whose feelings might be hurt.

Can I guarantee the deal would have been won had only the most expert of personnel been properly engaged? Of course not. However, I have no doubt the potential for the most successful outcome would have increased dramatically, as we could have had a rich discussion with a detailed focus on the capabilities specifically aligned to customer needs.

The teams that work for me know I follow a very simple rule when it comes to deals: "It is about winning, not about the individuals." What does that actually mean? I keep what I refer to as a skills matrix for my team, similar to the one shown in Table 4. Some companies create these matrices for their pool of technical resources, but I also keep one for my sales personnel.

TABLE 4: SKILLS MATRIX

	RANK	SOLUTION STRENGTH	INDUSTRY STRENGTH	MARKET SEGMENT	GLOBAL / DOM
SELLER 1	1	Infrastructure	Financial	Enterprise	Global
	2	End User Computing (MACD/BF)	Pharma		
	3	Cloud	Healthcare		
SELLER 2	1	Networking LAN / WAN	Manufacturing	Enterprise	International
	2	Data Center, Storage & Backup	Insurance	Commercial	Domestic
	3	Service Desk	Professional Services	Mid Market	Global
SELLER 3	1	Infrastructure, Networking LAN / WAN	Pharmaceutical	Enterprise	Global
	2	Service Desk	Finance	Commercial	International
	3	Cloud	Retail	Mid Market	
SELLER 4	1	Data Center	Manufacturing	Enterprise	Global
	2	End User Computing (MACD/BF)	Services	Commercial	International
	3	Network	Energy/Utilities	Mid Market	Domestic
SELLER 5	1	Data Center	Manufacturing	Enterprise	Global
	2	Networking/Communication	Technology	Enterprise	International
	3	Cloud	Aerospace/ Defense	Enterprise	Domestic
SELLER 6	1	Infrastructure Networking	Pharmaceutical	Enterprise	Global
	2	Data Center (Servers, Storage, Backup)	Healthcare	Commercial	International
	3	Service Desk	Manufacturing	Mid Market	Domestic
SELLER 7	1	Data Center	Financial	Enterprise	Global
	2	Service Desk, End User Compute (MACD/BF)	Manufacturing	Commercial	International
	3	Cloud	Retail	Mid Market	Domestic

If sellers have defined accounts within a territory or geography, why is this breakdown needed? The matrix enables me to make the best determination about skilled resources based on individual strengths. While sellers in many companies are defined by geography, that should not restrict the ability for a sales leader to make a judgment call to align a new opportunity to the individual with the greatest potential to win the engagement; it should not be assigned solely based on it being in the lesser-skilled seller's geographical area. If nothing else, a second seller with stronger skills could be assigned to assist the first, thus ensuring that properly skilled personnel are at least providing oversight. Again, this is about winning, not the individual. When applied often enough, all sellers have similar opportunities to take on deals in other regions, so it balances out across the team.

When reviewing the matrix, note that all columns are determined by a stack ranking by strength in that respective area. For sellers I track their individual area of solution expertise, industry strength, market strength, and possibly their background in working on global deals that require knowledge of taxation, conversion rates, shipping matters, and other specialized factors. I appreciate that for many this may seem unnecessary, as most leaders feel they know their people well enough; but when you are dealing with large engagements with numerous levels of complexity, it helps to weed through the tall grass and focus on what matters most. Plus, since the sellers actually provide the input for the matrix, they can't debate your decision when it becomes necessary.

My point is simple: never assume, and always inspect the facts more closely. Those tasked with leading the business have the most important responsibility to the success of the strategy we defined within the previous chapter. Sales leaders span across a broader breadth of field sellers, customers, and partners, and if they do not fully support, believe, or understand how to apply the strategy as defined, it will become a failing point that could weaken the success of the company. In that case, it becomes important to review the strategy with the leader again as a means of gaining their full understanding and commitment to the expectations. If they cannot align, you may need to take steps to get a more aligned leader in the role before your plans fall short. This may be harsh, I know, but nothing is more critical to the plan's success than the role the leader plays.

Employee Story 5: Excuses, Excuses, Excuses

I worked for a technology company for years. From the first day, I joined one of the biggest initiatives of the business, which was to grow our services practice. Year after year the sellers we tasked with selling our managed services offering, which the company spent millions of dollars over several years to develop. This was built into every individual's compensation plans and regional business plans, and was a major theme at the annual conference every year.

Yet the service never grew as much as the pool of excuses about why we could not sell it. The reality was that the sales leadership in the business was built of individuals accustomed to selling products, not services. They hired employees who had similar skills and beliefs as their own, and they trained and managed them based on their own personal knowledge—and worst of all, their own beliefs. Services was not part of that philosophy, and as a result it stagnated. Yet within the regions where a sales leader skilled with a service background aligned with that of the service strategy, the services base of business grew exponentially.

I am not stating that all sales leaders are at fault when a seller fails. I am posing the notion, however, that executives often limit their vision of fault to those individuals who carry the responsibility of the actual sale. Sellers do own responsibility for pulling all the right pieces together to ensure a sale is best positioned for a win, and they need to possess the proper skills to identity opportunities, develop a strong pipeline, build trusting relationships and yes, win deals. But when a seller is unsuccessful in achieving their goals, we need to look at the many elements that were in place and that could have contributed to their failure.

Employee Story 6: Commitment Issues

I was hired to assess and drive the new business strategy for a struggling business. The core business had for years been a product based offering with services attached, but the past two years had involved an initiative to transition to a services- and solutions-led business. This would allow for business expansion, as opposed to the commoditized shift within the product sales they had experienced.

Two years into the strategy, the product business continued to stagnate at even greater rates, and the existing base of services contracts experienced similar change. Why? The strategy was poorly defined, and it was being administered by the same leaders responsible for product sales, who lacked any experience with a service- or solution-led business model. Additionally, there many employees across the business displayed a lack of commitment to and enthusiasm for the direction in which the business was moving. The leaders had defined a strategy with little knowledge of how the business worked, then refused to commit wholeheartedly to it—and these people were responsible for communicating the message and inspiring an invigorating culture of change. All these elements can be breaking points for a business. Most businesses have one or two rights that need to be corrected; this company had needed to change almost all of them.

Could the business recover? Absolutely. The greatest benefit the business had at its disposal was an existing base of employees, beyond the leadership, who aspire to be successful and grow the business. The employees asked repeatedly how they could help and what role they could play. They simply lacked a well-defined vision, a strategy for success, and a leadership team with the proper knowledge and commitment to lead them through the storm. The ambitious employees strove to work harder and improve their outcomes, yet their changes were less effective, because they were individual changes rather than aligned initiatives for collaborative companywide success. In such cases, the leadership needs to be evaluated, not the employees.

If you are a newly established business or business unit, you have the ability to start fresh and make the right choices when hiring new sales leaders to create and drive the strategy. This can actually be a big advantage; without being distracted by long-term employees and existing methods, you can select based solely on which candidates' capabilities are aligned with your defined strategy and goals. This also adds great value to the new leader, who has the freedom to hire their own sellers to drive sales effectiveness.

If you are experiencing this situation within a currently established business, I recommend you take a close look at your leadership team and assess their alignment to your long-term strategy as a company. This can be difficult, as it is necessary to move past friendships and emotional ties and judge purely on skill and style. Even leaders' past successes must be overlooked; in essence, you should view them as new candidates for their role, as they are now employing a totally different strategy.

If you are an employee, especially a seller, I recommend that you work for an organization that not only markets the right culture and values in their approach to selling on their website, but demonstrates that commitment within the planning and actions of the sales leadership. For the recommendations in this book to work, sellers must have the full support of their sales leaders.

Let's face it: change is hard. But with self-awareness and alignment to a smart strategy, your business can achieve unprecedented success.

Chapter 9

THE RIGHT PEOPLE MAKE A WORLD OF DIFFERENCE
Changing Business Outcomes by Hiring for Results

THE RIGHT STRATEGIC PLANS are complete and the right leaders are in place; now it is time to assess the people who are going to make all the work that went into the planning a huge success. As a sales leader, tough decisions are ahead regardless of whether your team of sellers is already established or you are interviewing candidates.

While those who have an established team are likely taking a deep breath and feeling a sense of relief that all you have to do is hold a team meeting, share the plan concepts, assign a quota and off the team goes to find new sales, I am going to request you hit the pause button now and recommend a possible reset in your thinking before continuing on. I'm going to put it out there: you will most likely need to hire new sellers either way.

Why is a pause necessary? If you've worked with members of this team for long enough, you may feel you're ready to go sell. But are you? Have you truly assessed the corporate strategy behind the various business plans and matched them against the skills of your individual sellers, or have you simply decided to forge ahead with the existing team because it's easier? After all, believing that the people we already have are the right ones is certainly easier than recruiting and interviewing candidates who could very well turn out to be worse. Sales leaders can also certainly have a weakness for their teams, especially if they hired most of the sellers themselves.

This type of loyalty is a noble weakness, but a weakness nonetheless. You must pause and consider the reality that your team might not be the most capable one to help you reach your highest level of business or financial outcome. You might get to 101% attainment, but if you can achieve 140% attainment simply by making better choices, why wouldn't you want to? Let's work through our options.

When to Rely on Existing Employees

I have always found success by focusing on the strategic plan end goal and not simply confusing those goals with the emotions of the people I developed relationships with. It sounds sort of cold when I say it, but I don't mean it that way at all. I worked closely with every seller to better understand their skills and how they matched to the strategic expectations of how we planned to grow the business. Nothing here was done in a vacuum.

While continuing forward with your current team may get you to that 101% initially, it may backfire when a new strategic plan is introduced. The same team may drop to 50% attainment if they are unable to adjust to the newly defined strategic model. It is a sales leader's job to assess whether the sellers' backgrounds provide enough in terms of selling strengths to change from their current way of selling to the new strategy. Sales leaders should not just assume this transition will work but rather properly evaluate the many rights of the business and take action for change as necessary.

An easy example of this is the seller who has sold product and consistently overachieved in quota for several years; he is simply the best at fulfilling that type of customer need. Add this level of skill to an account base that seller has had for years, and the seller appears to have a can't-miss formula for achieving quota, as does his sales leader.

Yet now introduce a change in business strategy. His sales leader must shift toward selling a service. Most sales leaders trust that the experienced seller can adjust to selling services with his strong selling skills. The reality is that he likely cannot. Let me identify some common misconceptions and mistakes that can lead to leader failure.

Mistake 1: Having so much faith in the seller or team that it blinds your ability to see the truth. The truth will come out when your year-end numbers fall short; do your due diligence and challenge the sellers so that you can better understand their skill. Facing the problem prior to the inception of the year is the best way to assure your yearlong success. The longer you ignore or overlook the likely problem, the more your sales success will diminish with each month that passes.

Mistake 2: Believing that sales is sales, and if your best sellers can sell one type of offering they can sell them all. While I believe great sellers can transition or expand their skill, very few do it successfully. Fewer do it overnight. This is often due to their mindset and whether they believe in what they are tasked with selling. If you want to get an idea of who will or will not make the transition well, look at all your sellers' sales results for the past three years. Notice a trend in them selling one type of offering? This is especially easy to see if your company already offers a mix of product and services and certain sellers consistently sell one over the other. That shows what they know, trust, and believe in. Don't put blinders on and kid yourself into failure.

Mistake 3: Not listening. Your best sellers, if comfortable with you, will openly tell you if they do not like the new strategy or business model. They will also share their feelings with other team members, and this will inevitably come back your way through the rumor mill. Stop ignoring what you hear and address it quickly. When people speak out openly against the goals of your strategy, it should be a red flag.

Mistake 4: Ignoring the sellers' lack of desire to learn the new skills needed to sell the expanded offerings. Even if sellers do not say flat-out that they aren't interested in making the transition, many may find excuses or reasons not to learn. This will show up in your pipeline when no new deals are added for the new offerings. Don't ignore what is right before your eyes.

In "Chapter 6: Strategic Planning," I have written a section on financial planning that will allow you to see if a seller's fit is going to be a prosperous one. It is very easy to see, upon deeper review, if your seller has the attributes or desire to sell something different than what they have become accustomed to selling. Another indicator is whether their existing best customer base ever purchases anything beyond the products they order regularly. The reality is that a customer might only be buying product from you because of long-term customer discounts and the only offerings your seller actively discusses with the customer; they may have numerous other providers for the services element and will not plan to add you to that list of vendors. If your best seller has no history of selling anything other than a defined list of offerings and never shows the capability or desire to sell outside their comfort zone, I am confident that they will likely fail when you ask them to move in a new direction. If you do not pause and inspect the existing team now, you may experience a drop in sales and even a loss of existing customers. You can blame the company for changing the strategy, but you had the opportunity to plan and act in advance.

Again, I am not opposed to utilizing a current team if you have the proper level of confidence in them. I am simply asking that you pause, conduct the appropriate level of due diligence, and assess your situation honestly. As a leader, you own it and have the power to change it. You owe it to yourself, your team, your company, and that individual seller who will likely fail to identify the risk and address it. This is what leaders do.

When to Recruit and Rebuild

Recruiting is easy when you are building a newly established team or when you have an open headcount to fill. Unlike working with existing employees, you do not have to try and fit a square peg in a round hole; you can recruit for candidates that have the specific attributes and skills you are seeking to be most successful. You are thus afforded the luxury of controlling your own destiny. This is actually a powerful position to be in, and can lead to unlimited success if you have the will to wait for those who are the best fit. Best fit means best fit for the role, period, not best fit available at the time. Do not settle; be patient and be committed to what you expect in the right people you hire.

Your first step in the hiring process should be to completely rewrite the job description. This will allow you to communicate what is needed in a way that will attract the type of individual you know will excel in the role. By using specific keywords, you might attract different types and levels of talent than you have traditionally hired in the past.

I worked with a firm that was having difficulties hiring. They were looking for less experienced, highly trainable technical personnel who might be open to both a potentially lower pay scale than others in the industry and who would display an enthusiasm for learning new technologies as we expanded the product offerings. I recommended that we change the outdated job description they used as a standard post for that role. We added points about technologies that new college graduates or less experienced engineers might have interest in learning as a next step in their career; in addition to the traditional technologies they offered the market for years, we highlighted our emerging markets for cloud based services, mobility, automation and advanced robotics. Within a week we had more responses and a wider breadth of talent to select from than the company had received in past months. It was as simple as creating the right posting to uncover the right talent for the roles we needed to fill. A refresh of an outdated job requirement can reap tremendous benefits as opposed to the continued recycling of the same old message. Remember, people also want to evolve.

When seeking the right people, you have to trust your ability to identify the talent that makes sense and best fits the role expectation. One of the toughest things about having numerous open quota bearing positions is that your executives want them filled quickly so they can begin to sell immediately. This might work for some basic product-type sales roles, but it is certainly not the way to find the right people who will sell at the highest levels of success and remain with the company long term. This type of hiring often results in a revolving-door situation, where candidates who are not a good fit move on and other subpar candidates are recruited quickly to fill the space. Recruiting team members, even inside your own company, can be just as pushy when it comes to filling roles quickly; they too have quotas to fill and other roles to worry about. Do not let the pressure change your commitment to hiring the right people. This will be the difference between mediocrity (90%-101%) and excellence (greater than 120%) in your achievement of quota. Great leaders never settle.

This is a long process. It could take perhaps three months to find the right people that fit your plans, and upon hire those new employees may take three to six months to establish themselves and develop a potential pipeline that generates the level of success you expect. This means that you could be waiting approximately six to nine months before you see the level of attainment you were looking for—nearly a full fiscal year before knowing if they were the right or wrong choice for the role. This is why being patient and finding the right candidate is so essential. An extra few months is nothing if it will give your business the best potential for strong outcomes long term; it will serve you better than recruiting

> **This will be the difference between mediocrity (90%-101%) and excellence (greater than 120%) in your achievement of quota.**

and hiring the wrong employees every six months, especially when you take into account that no employee is reaching their maximum success rate in six months. That patience will pay off with long-term success for you, the company, and the new employee.

I will offer one last suggestion. It is not only a good recruiting practice, but it also put me as sales leader into the strongest possible position for achieving higher success. If an open headcount occurs, either due to a role being vacated or expansion, other sellers on the team will be quick to reach out and try to take on the top accounts left behind by the seller who has left the company. This is especially true if multiple people share territories. While it may frustrate the other sellers on the team, I strongly recommend that you do not reassign those accounts until you find a new person. Having that top account—the right customer—available may be a way to attract the right people with the right strengths. Remember, allocation of accounts is not about making reps happy; it is about aligning the right people with the right customers to better enable your plan to reach the greatest level of outcome for the company. When the company benefits as do the employees.

Consider what typically occurs when people vacate a role in a traditional sales structure. Let's say you have a team of five salespeople, each have been with the team for one year or more, and each have an existing account base. That account base is typically comprised of one to three base customers who generate a consistent revenue stream and then a list of new prospective customers being pursued (hunted). One or two of those five sellers are your top sellers; they each have one to two really great accounts. One of the top sellers leaves the team for a new role. Your remaining sellers pounce like a lion on a gazelle; they line up at your door pitching reasons that they should be the seller who manages that top customer.

If you agree and hand it over, you no longer have a carrot with which to attract a top seller away from your competitors and improve your team. You also now start to lose proper selling balance across your team; now all the best accounts are owned by two or three team members, and anyone you hire is coming into a pure hunting role. This means you will need to hire a seller with different skills than you might have wanted to support your strategy. All of this is not to mention that their success will not peak for at least 6-12 months, as pure hunting requires much more time for establishing customer relationships and a quality pipeline. The new sellers are more likely to get frustrated and leave due to the lack of active business and commissions or perceived inequality on the team. You might as well have them sign a 90-day performance plan when they start, as they're being set up to fail from the beginning. Obviously, this is a joke (and one that doesn't always go over well when I tell it to executives), but in all seriousness, success does not come from making the easy choices. It comes from making the right choices that lead to increased success and not backing down.

Could it be possible that allowing an experienced employee to take over a best customer is better than having someone new take them? Of course. But if you give an existing team member one of the top accounts left behind, they should give up one of their existing customers in exchange. This might be a good way to best match seller skills with the right customers in your scenario. But if you are handing a prime account to a current seller for reasons of ease or to do them a favor, consider the ramifications. You can potentially diminish both your talent pool for recruitment and your potential financial outcomes if they do not have the skills to gain the highest possible results. Always think in terms of what aligns best to your right strategic plan and craft a team that will be successful.

Successful Sellers Have Certain Right Traits

The best sellers not only understand but live by key characteristics. When those characteristics exist, the rights of selling have the greatest potential to meet the expectations of the right strategy. The following attributes are shared by top sellers:

They say no: Top sellers say no to customers, no to deals that do not align with their company strengths, no to submitting a proposal of poor quality, no to pursuing a deal they know they will lose just because they are afraid of not proposing anything, no to golf outings when quotas have not been met, and more if necessary.

They personalize every response to every customer: Using a standard proposal and presentation will result in an unimpressed *no* from the customer almost every time. But submitting a personalized proposal or presentation that clearly articulates and demonstrates how that customer will benefit is of utmost value to the customer. Customers need to see exactly how what is being proposed will positively impact their existing business. Make it personalized. Good sellers understand that differentiation wins.

They never believe that the customer is their friend: It is a mistake to believe that a customer's business is guaranteed because of a perceived friendship. Even when a relationship is strong, approach every engagement as if it were the first with that customer. Let down your guard or get too comfortable and you lose.

They never become complacent: Spend time building new relationships with those working for existing customers, and net new customer acquisition every day. Customers' buying patterns can shift overnight. Do not get caught by surprise and have to start over without warning or new contacts.

They are smart about prospecting: The best sellers focus their time on customers that fit the key qualifications of the offerings they sell and how their company does business. Learn about a prospective customer before you prospect.

They sell value, not just a discounted price: Understand why your solution is of value to the customer and how it differentiates from competitors' offerings and discounting will not be necessary. Once you become known as a discounter, it only puts your success at risk. You become judged solely on pricing, and a large pool of competitors is waiting in the wings to push you out. Most customers are looking for value over discount.

Focus your efforts on what matters. Spend your time as if you have little of it and focus your resources, work efforts, and thought processes on what will build stronger relationships and win more deals.

Aligning to the Plan

The right people are only right if they fully understand and support the strategy you expect to achieve your outcomes and success. If you have existing or new team members being considered and they lack skill, do not have a history of success in selling what your plan is focused on selling, or do not have the proper people skills or winning attitude, I recommend you continue the search for the right people.

Do not underestimate the impact the right people will have on your team's success. People can make the difference between achieving an attainment of 101%, 150%, or 50%. Expand that thinking to financial outcome and consider the impact an incorrectly aligned seller can make on customer outcomes. The right people who embrace the right strategic plan enable the right customers to expand and prosper with little if any customer satisfaction issues. You earn top dollars in new sales and simultaneously suffer no lost earnings from time spent on avoidable issues. Conversely, a seller who was assigned as a favor or hired to fill the headcount gap might appear at a high level to just be behind on the sales numbers can damage both sales and customer relationships. It can be difficult to tell how much damage a new hire is really doing for several months, as they are still within their initial learning period. In the meantime, you have dissatisfied customers who are spending less with you—and more with your competitors. Pay attention to your sales team's alignment with your strategic plan and you can avoid these risks.

Let me share two brief stories on this subject. Both are direct experiences I have had with sellers and customers within companies I have assisted.

Employee Story 7: Friends without Benefits

I joined an established organization with a team of sellers already in place. About a year into the role, having met all the primary customers and establishing the business plan and sales GTM, I decided to reassign our top revenue-spending customer from the existing seller they had worked with for seven years to a different seller.

My reasoning was that, upon speaking with the customer about their business needs on multiple occasions, and having discussed strategy with the long-time seller, the seller seemed to be thinking for the customer as opposed to thinking like the customer. This is an important distinction. It is fine for a seller to think like a customer, as it creates synergy between the seller and the customer experience, allowing the seller to properly anticipate the customer's needs, and helps the seller to be more proactive and supportive. On the contrary, a seller who begins to think for the customer makes decisions on their behalf. They take responsibility for deciding what the customer will or will not be interested in before ever introducing the new product or capabilities to that customer. This often occurs when a seller has worked the same account for too long. The result is that as a company, you no longer appear innovative to the customer or focused on their long-term needs, and the relationship and spending begins to flatten. It is as though the seller is simply showing up to pick up POs but offering nothing further in terms of innovation or creative thinking. The seller is complacent.

However, there was a challenge here. The primary contact at the customer, the director of IT, had become personal friends with the existing seller, so now they had more than just a business relationship tying them together. When I informed them both that I was making the change, the director was quick to tell me of his personal friendship with the seller and share with me that if the seller left for a competitor as a result of the switch, he would move with him. I told him that I respected his feedback but was making the change to improve his ability to expand his own business, improve his satisfaction levels, and help provide a broader view of capabilities that could change his future. I promised him that the change was being made for the right reasons and that he would see the benefits very soon. He thanked me and told me he would give it a chance, but reiterated that he was disappointed.

Later in the year, following our annual review session, I attended dinner with that customer and his team. I was on guard for a potential ass chewing, but he was quick to smile and shake my hand. He said: "I have to tell you—I have never been supported by a rep as well as our new rep has supported us. He has done a great job and introduced us to some tools that seem like they can really improve my business. I know I was skeptical, but it is working out very well. Thanks!"

Apparently customer satisfaction had never been better—but what did the numbers say? Upon review, I saw that sales to that customer had increased that year by 15%. Enough said.

Employee Story 8: "What Happened to the $26M?"

I was visiting our California office to meet with some customers. One of the sellers from another division was conducting a quarterly account review. As an executive for the company, I was asked to join if I had the time. The first slide the seller presented depicted a sales timeline for a customer. It showed that the customer had spent $18M with our company in 2012, $26M in 2013, $35M in 2014—and $9M in 2015.

The people in the room asked a few product-related questions and the seller went on to the next slide. I quickly asked that we return to the last slide, as I had a question: "What happened to the $26M?"

Confused looks all around. I elaborated: the customer had increased their spending every year for the past three years, and yet this past fiscal year they had spent $26M less than the previous. "Who are they spending it with?"

His response was: "No one. They are on a spending freeze and are not spending any money on technology this year."

While I understand that customers can have spending cutbacks, I also know that when it came to the type of technology my company sold, customers could not just stop spending. Doing so would greatly impact their environment and user base. This was also a Fortune 500 account, and they were growing in the market. "Do you know who else the customer used as a vendor?"

"I don't know," the seller responded.

"Have you reached out to the manufacturer, who speaks to the customer regularly, to see if they have filled other orders for that customer themselves or through another vendor?"

"No."

"Okay. When the customer does buy equipment, do you ask what they use it for—meaning what problem are they incurring and trying to solve?"

"No." His tone was growing frustrated.

"You are responsible for what has developed into a $35M customer for the company. They are now a $9M customer. I believe it is in all our best interest to know what has changed and how we can improve the situation." I decided to end the conversation there, but inquired with sales leaders about the seller after the meeting had ended. They told me that he had been on that account for exactly one year.

To any sales leaders reading this scenario: I hope alarm bells are going off. The largest customer in a region spending significantly less within the same period of time a new seller was assigned to the account? This is a red flag. In addition, the seller had supported this one and only customer for a year, he did not even know who he was competing against? He had never engaged with the customer to better understand their buying needs? This was not a seller who was embracing the strategy that had been created or respected the right customer. More concerning for me was that even after being told about a loss of $26M in revenue, the sales leader did not ask a single question. When pressed, they all simply pointed fingers at the partners and customer.

In both of the above scenarios, the right people were not in the right roles nor working with the right customers, yet they retained their assigned accounts. In Employee Story 7, it was because he had always been the seller on the account. In Employee Story 8, the seller was assigned most likely because he lobbied for the customer during a time of transition—yet the sales leader never bothered to look more deeply into the erosion of $26M of business in a single year. The fact that this did not raise an alarm for either tells us there was definitely a problem with both individuals having these roles.

I would be remiss to not mention such areas as compensation related to people. Look to Chapter 14 in this book, which covers the right quota for the compensation discussion. Do not overlook the need for alignment to compensation models for your sellers and sales leaders. I am not a big proponent of the compensation plan and quota becoming the pseudo-sales leader, as happens in many organizations, but it is a powerful driver of sales expectations. It needs to be complimentary to the overall corporate strategy, goals, and objectives you define, as well as properly balanced across all the business units that play a supporting role for the right customers.

Right Team

As Duke basketball coach Mike Krzyzewski so eloquently put it, "I get a group of people who are talented to commit to excellence and to work together as one. That's where it starts. Different talents, same commitment."

Coach K. makes the final point of my right people chapter. The most valuable asset you can have is a team of people who work together to create success. Sellers have a bad reputation for caring about themselves—just look at the villainous salesmen in the movies—but the myth of sellers lying, cheating, and stealing from their own team members is rarer than it seems. My experience has always been that teams built with the right people thrive. Sometimes you do hire a square peg for a round hole, but that becomes evident fairly quickly, and if mismatches are resolved in a timely manner disaster can be averted. Having all the rights discussed in this book in place will help filter out individuals who might not blend well with the rest of the team.

When a team is properly constructed, the unity in accomplishing goals and initiatives and the level of support and sharing can be amazing. I have been fortunate to be part of teams that openly offer one another assistance with deals and share ideas to help other team members sell. When teams work together as one, as Coach K. stated, your rights can accelerate your success beyond your expectations. Focus your time on interviewing new team members beyond their individual sales skills; look closely at their ability to be part of a team and enhance the culture within the business. Ask team-focused questions during the interview process and when speaking to their references. It will make a difference.

You now have the right people, the right strategy, and the right leadership. Now you need to create a winning formula for how your team can work together as one.

Chapter 10

COMBINING PLANS AND PEOPLE WITH THE RIGHT CUSTOMERS
Aim for the Bottom, Get the Bottom; Aim for the Top, Win

YOU HAVE DEFINED THE RIGHT STRATEGY for your success, appointed the right leaders in key roles, and hired the right people in other supporting roles such as sales, marketing, delivery, R&D, finance, and HR. Now let's go make money!

Wait, not quite yet. We know what we want to sell and to whom, but do we really know who will make the decision to purchase from us instead of the competition? More importantly, do we know with greater certainty which customers will recognize us as a leader in our industry and demand we be their partner? What seller would not want the customer fighting to work with us, as opposed to having to fight to make a sale? This important step in the process will help you continue to improve your odds.

Let me begin with a reflection on my own experience rebuilding a business with a focus on customer base. I accepted a role in a new organization leading a region that I had never worked with before. I had little broad knowledge of the potential customers in that market. Fortunately, the organization I had joined was an established organization with a large customer base—but unfortunately, it was also in a state of flux. The business was in the middle of combining three different smaller business acquisitions into a single regional technology company with common goals. I quickly realized that my role as sales leader and GM was to listen before all else so that I could understand what was and was not working. I spent my days and nights studying the market, learning about the skills of my sales team, analyzing financial data, and of course learning about the current customer base and what made them choose us over the regional competition. We were selling an array of IT infrastructure, such as network and services, so the people I was working to establish relationships with were IT directors and their direct team of technical engineers, VPs, and some CxO-level executives. Coming from the same industry, I considered all this normal.

However, something abnormal soon emerged. I was being asked to speak with an inordinate amount of unhappy customers to rectify levels of dissatisfaction with our inability to meet their needs as promised. Most businesses in this industry may incur such challenges once or twice per month at most; these complaints were coming in multiple times a week. The level of dissatisfaction and negative feedback were consistent among every customer I spoke with; it was so bad that even our top manufacturing partners were inviting competitors to meet the customers and bid against us. In addition, a number of salespeople from my team were complaining about the support challenges they faced that threatened their ability to retain customers.

It's never good to have unhappy customers, but their complaints greatly improved my ability to gather data and assess what was wrong. This meant I needed to take action prior to even finishing my assessment of the business and properly applying my methodology to sales effectiveness (which I'll discuss shortly). However, it did afford me the opportunity to prove that my principles worked in small ways even prior to the grander methods being activated. The opportunity for small successes had come out of what seemed to be a big problem.

It was clear that my new company simply did not serve the customers at the level they expected. What were the issues?

1. My company was focused very heavily on growing the enterprise- and large commercial-grade customers within the infrastructure marketplace. This means our goals as an organization were more heavily driven to customers who had, at that time, 700 or more end users. The customers with complaints were SMB or small commercial companies (this means customers with well below 700 end users in market terms). While these smaller customers had likely been a good match in earlier years, they were soon no longer within the company's business model as their focus customer. Because of that growth and changing strategic direction, when issues popped up, the business was quick to reallocate resources supporting our smaller customers and prioritize the needs of the larger customer instead. Thus, the smaller customer was left waiting for assistance for what often turned into extended periods of time and their own unmet business obligations.

2. Additionally, I soon found that sellers were agreeing to provide services related to technical capabilities that we did not even possess at the time and were outside our defined areas of specialization. While this seemed to be a necessity when

growing a business, it was no longer possible; still, sellers felt compelled to say "yes" to avoid losing the business. All too often, this resulted in a resource skilled in a completely different technical specialty going to the customer site with a handbook on how to support the technology. (If you've never been in this situation before, I can tell you with certainty that customers do not like seeing resources they've paid high price for reading a how-to manual on site.)

3. Finally, as the business grew, so did the business budgets, the quotas allocated to sellers, and the costs to provide the service. Accordingly, the hourly rates billed to customers also grew. The SMB and small commercial customers were unable to pay these prices—or unwilling to pay them for such poor service.

Unfortunately for those customers and my sellers, I recognized that eventually we needed to stop being the provider of choice for these smaller customers. They were not bad customers, and nothing they were requesting was unreasonable; my company was simply no longer the right fit for their business needs. As the new sales leader and GM, I realized early the need to instill controls in the selling methodology.

If we had so much business, why couldn't we just hire new resources and take care of all the customers the same way? It's a valid question, but it would have been a temporary fix and would not have solved our problem long term. The fact remained that our business model and strategy were evolving, and it was in the best interest of the employees within my company to clearly understand how that would affect the way they supported customers moving forward. It was also our responsibility to properly educate the customer on how they would be better supported by a different business model.

How did we reallocate these customers without making it feel as though we were "firing" them? We offered them options. The customers who desired to remain with us had the option to receive proposals for technology via an inside proposal team, not the field-based sellers. The fact is that as a larger technology reseller, we had better discounts than other providers. We were still able to resell technology at a favorable price, but utilizing an inside proposal team afforded us improved margins to support smaller purchases. Those same customers could decide whether they still wanted to utilize our company for services—with the understanding that our hourly rates had increased and resource allocation would be "as available" based on our enterprise and large commercial customer focus. We also created a defined list of products and services we would sell and support, and remained focused solely on those offerings so we could be recognized as a leader in those technologies without deviating into one-off products we could not fully support or follow through on.

All this was needed simply to decrease our challenges with existing dissatisfied customers. We still needed to proactively redefine which customers would best accelerate our effectiveness and grow our revenue base and profit while also ensuring a good living for our employees. My approach was what I refer to as the *less is more* method. I firmly believe this method is the best way to generate higher levels of customer loyalty and sales outcomes, and it has proven highly effective for the sales teams I have led.

Less is More Method

Let me get right to the point. Would you rather have 10 POs or 4? Ask that question of your team. Your best and brightest sellers might ask about the value of each PO before they commit to an answer. I focus my leadership style and sales modeling strongly on my belief that having less is better than having more; that being said, defining the right choices are what makes that model a success. Unfortunately, many people within our society and within the sales community, even executives, have the gut reaction that quantity matters most. This thinking pervades the transactional business environment every day; yet I see little value in quantity if it is not backed up by quality and the benefit of time.

Let's go back to the original question, but this time I'll add a twist. Would you rather have 10 pennies or 4 quarters? It's a different number of coins, and an even more different result. Heck, I could change the example from pennies to nickels and you would still receive no greater benefit by having more. In fact, let's dive deeper—into the cost of producing the coins themselves. In 2014, the US Mint reported that the cost of producing a penny was approximately 1.8 cents, and the cost of a nickel was 9.4 cents. Yet the cost of producing a quarter, which is worth much more, was 11 cents. That's right: our government is losing money every time we produce the lesser-valued coin.

Don't be too surprised: as salespeople, you are likely accepting POs that have the same negative impact on your company (although you don't notice, since you keep receiving them and getting paid commission on them). Those who focus all their time and effort on smaller POs without adding in larger deals contribute to higher production costs and risk the region or company's ability to be profitable overall. The consistency of receiving this type of PO may feel good, but you're ultimately putting yourself, your company and customer at risk.

So it pays, quite literally, to apply improved logic for identifying the right customers who will be cutting the PO. We work equally hard to get any PO, no matter the size—so why not get a quarter-sized PO instead of a bunch that add up like pennies? If you want to help your team and company reach the greatest levels of success, you need to start better defining your preferred customer base and those deals that make most sense to pursue—those that generate quarters or even dimes.

The penny-and-quarter idea applies across all companies that sell a good or service, not just larger corporations. I realize that some businesses exist for the purpose of fulfilling business needs for customers with a small level of need, which also leads to smaller orders or POs. In this situation, it's essential to know whether your business is modeled the right way to be able to support the costs associated with selling to smaller customers. A wealth of goods and services providers exists today, and the resources of each are designed to support a specific customer base. Sellers and sales leaders just need to better understand which customer is best suited for their results and focus in that area.

What I am about to propose might require change and additional discipline in the manner in which you sell to and support your customer base. Most sellers or sales leaders already do it to some level, so it will not be impossible to accomplish, but it needs to be applied across all customers. While it may be uncomfortable to commit to applying my approach universally, when you do so the benefits will be enormous—for you, your company, and most importantly, your customers. Selling is not about how much you do, but about the quality of your work and knowing where best to spend your time. Make it count. I have worked by this approach as both a salesperson and sales leader at multiple companies and have never failed at reaching the highest possible financial benefits. Moreover, when

> **❝ Selling is not about how much you do, but about the quality of your work and knowing where best to spend your time. Make it count.❞**

followed thoroughly this selling philosophy will add to customer loyalty, strengthen your partnerships with providers and manufacturers, and even improve your quality of life.

It is important to realize that results will not come overnight. However, monitoring small progress points and having patience will make all the difference. Only a small portion of the sales team will align quickly, likely because they already have the top customers in the company assigned to them and this model appears to change nothing for them. Many, however, will question the rationale. Those who believe in having 30, 40, or 50 customers assigned to them will see little value in this approach, because they trust in the power of quantity before quality—they like the sound of a lot of pennies or nickels jingling in their pocket. For them, more is better; even their smallest customer is important because they feel good about that more frequent yet smaller PO to validate their efforts. But a smaller PO does not equal success; in fact, that wasted time and effort may even cost you a bigger PO down the line. My approach will teach you how best to utilize each type of seller and your own time.

Less is More in Practice

Let's return to the story about the technology reseller I joined years ago. To recap, that business was growing, yet struggling to provide clear value to their customers and partners. Selling activities appeared strong, but the volume of activity[2] based on many smaller deals was overwhelming the current sales and delivery teams. Yet they were also expanding their customer base to larger enterprise-based customers.

---

2   As a quick clarification, the use of the word *activity* for a seller can include phone calls, emails, quotes, re-quotes, driving to the customer (windshield time), planning with technical resources, planning with partners, forecast calls, RFQ/RFP responses, and more.

Sales began to stagnate and customer satisfaction was escalating to a boiling point for all involved.

At the time, we had 5 salespeople within a region with 310 active customers. "Active customer" means that the customer had provided us with a PO of any dollar value within the previous 12 months. All 5 salespeople were invited in for a full 2-day session to review their assigned account base. This session was more about the positioning within the account—meaning how much they spent annually, how many contacts we knew within the account, contact roles, partner synergy, and why they aligned to our business objectives. These are the basic elements most teams discuss related to their accounts. We avoided discussing customer satisfaction in this session. My reasons for this were simple: I needed to know little more than the fact that we had 5 salespeople supporting 310 customers to know we had dissatisfied customers and a less than desirable win rate. So when the aforementioned customer issues came up, it was no surprise. I also knew that with the less-is-more groundwork I was beginning to do, customer satisfaction soon wouldn't be an issue.

To begin, it's important to understand some level of selling metrics for your business. Don't get too bogged down by metrics; this will only result in analysis paralysis. I say this as a person who loves statistics and data for making good decisions: For this foundational effort, keep it simple.

The following information held the most value in this session:

- **Total percent of revenue each individual customer represents (divide customer generated revenue by total sales revenue)**
    - » It is helpful to know how they rank in terms of total revenue.

- **Total percent of gross profit each individual customer represents (divide customer generated gross profit by total sales gross profit)**
    - » Again, it is nice to know how they rank, especially as rank for profitability can be quite different than rank for total revenue. I look for profitable customers more than I do big revenue generators with little to no profit. I will discuss this in more depth later.
- **Three-year purchasing history per customer**
    - » Do not overlook anything. In a technology company we would look separately at technology, professional services, managed services, and rebate potential. Additionally, look separately at different areas of specialty within your business portfolio of offerings, such as networking, data center, call center, security, etc.
    - » History demonstrates customer loyalty, profitability potential, growth within customer, buying patterns (specific to refreshes and projects), wallet share, etc.
- **Distribution of customers between sales personnel**
- **Total number of businesses within the geographic region**
    - » Look also to see how many of those businesses have headquarters within the region.
- If available, include your key partners' and manufacturers' customer lists to show the level of importance to their business
    - » This can also identify prospective customers you may need to add to your list for future acquisition.

You can add as much data as you would like, but these provide me ample information to begin making choices.

Again, too much data and overview will be detrimental to the task at hand. Keep it clear and keep it crisp and avoid analysis paralysis. Another important element of good analysis is to keep your own personal ideals out of the assessment. When reviewing data, just assess the results the data depicts related to business strategy success without letting your emotions playing a role or expecting people to see the data from your point of view. It is important to know your strengths when it comes to data analysis and how to disseminate the information correctly. I consider myself strong in assessing fluctuation and identifying outliers; if this is not a strong point for you, you should feel comfortable getting other team members' input as needed.

Now that you have your data, what do you do with it? First and foremost, be sure you know what matters most to your business. The company strategy is relevant here, as are the goals and objectives you created at the seller or sales leader level to achieve the strategy. As GM, gross profit per customer was critical to my success, as it was a key measurement for the company, and customer relationship was very important to how I run my model. The smaller the total profit for an individual customer, the less effort I could afford to apply to that customer for long-term success. This also meant I risked having a decreased level of customer satisfaction, which could lead to a weakened relationship overall. Thus my two most important elements, profit and customer satisfaction, had to be properly balanced.

How do we put the plan into action? The following are keys to successful implementation of a new model within a business.

- **Communication, communication, communication**
    » The potential for change of any kind will never be successful without communicating your purpose, your plan for implementation, and your desired outcomes of

success, whether those be financial or goal-based. This needs to be done at all levels of the organization.
   » Sellers will be most interested in how this potential for change can positively impact their ability to earn. Know your audience and the key points that have the most meaning for them personally.
- **Start off with one salesperson at a time if necessary as a way to demonstrate the initiatives can lead to desired outcomes.**
- **Identify areas along the way where the less is more plan might best begin to be implemented.** Nothing needs to be discussed during this two-day session, just documented for your purposes later.
- **Find the salesperson on the team who you feel will best follow a new model.**
   » Make sure they also have the most to gain.
   » Choose a salesperson who has the respect of other team members.
- **Review salesperson's existing account list.** Take time to review historical purchases from customers and their individual strengths—of all the offerings you sell, what do they excel in?

The two-day session should uncover several things for you as a seller or sales leader. The most important: Are the customers you are currently assigned to and/or targeting best aligned to what your company capabilities are and the level of success you wish to achieve? If the answer to either is no, move that customer to the side for now; if the answer is maybe, look a little closer and make a call about whether to keep them on the list or remove them. This is not an emotional exercise; keep your focus on which prospective customers make the most sense and which do not. After all, you are doing this for the benefit of the customer as much as for your benefit as a vendor of goods and services. This is not an exercise in finding the most money; it is also a way to identify those customers that will reap the greatest benefit from their relationship with you.

I caution you that sellers often cling to their closest customers, regardless of future potential or not. Just because a customer speaks to you does not make them a potential for great sales. The actual account as a whole must be considered, not just the individual contact the seller is speaking with. Far too often, the seller is not even speaking with the proper contact anyway, just the most talkative contact. The goal is to identify those customers that best fit your strategy, will recognize the greatest value, will enable you to expand your relationships and grow stronger within the account, and of course will allow for profitable outcomes.

Keep it fresh. Salespeople who are on the same account longer than 3-5 years may need to be reassigned, as their ability to be highly effective has likely changed. They will not admit that to be the case, but it is important to know when this has occurred and act accordingly.

Making Smarter Decisions

I mentioned earlier that the team I worked with had 310 active customers. The goal was to reduce this number to one that made sense for my business' desired margin and fit my need for better customer relationships. I did not define a goal at the beginning of the meeting with the team—say, reducing the number of customers in the region from 310 to 150. That was not the intention of the work session, nor would it have gained the results I wanted. A number is not the goal. The goal is to assess the customer base as a team and watch the team rationalize the way their customers fit within the strategy, goals, and objectives of the business. The goal was to show them why reaching out to some customers makes more sense than reaching out to others. The result of the work leads to an account base that makes the most sense to achieve the expected outcomes.

For two days we scrubbed each customer, categorizing them by geographic location, current spend, user base, their relation to the market, the technology that ran their business environment, the vendors they used (if we knew that information), and other relevant details. We also assessed why our company was a good fit for supporting each customer's business and how our partners or manufacturers would or would not assist us in growing that customer relationship. Partners can be a big factor in this scenario, as they also work with other vendors and may not have the desire to disrupt what they are doing with another vendor so that you can engage more deeply in a customer.

As I would have expected, the two days were filled with sellers selling me on why they like certain customers they were used to working with today. I repeatedly responded: "Stop being concerned about pitching me on your customers, and let's get back to assessing their value as a customer."

The two days resulted in a team that was much more educated about their regional business environment. We didn't reduce our numbers down to that 150 I mentioned earlier; I never thought we would. Change takes time—not only in actual application of effort, but even more so in mentality and confidence. My comfort was in seeing that by the end of the two-day session, the team could tell me which customers did or did not make sense. That was the progress I was looking for in this initial meeting.

The work the team and I were doing to change the regional business progressed every day for the next three years. *Every day* means I continually reinforced my message and approach in every individual discussion with sellers, every pipeline review, every quarterly review, every executive discussion, every partner meeting...every day, period. If it was going to work, it had to be what I believed in as a sales leader and GM above all else. The model started as it usually does, with one seller, evolved to two sellers, and finally spread across the entire team. What is it they say in the military—you will win the war one battle at a time?

As Table 5 demonstrates, the model worked. It took the natural course of time to see the results, along with a high level of patience and focus on quality, but the results were staggering. Did it work because of my leadership? Yes. But that was only part of it. Would it have worked with only my leadership? No. It worked because the rights I discuss throughout the book were all being applied and supported throughout the business. My messaging supported a model I fully believed in with a company that allowed me to apply the model against a broader strategy. The executive team played a major role in supporting my direction, as did all the sellers, supporting resources, other business units, the partners, and of course the customers. The model worked and worked at the highest level as defined due to all the many parts being applied properly and accepted amongst all involved.

TABLE 5: 3 YEAR RESULTS

	DAY ONE	AFTER 3 YEARS
ACTIVE CLIENTS	Began with 310 active clients covered by 5 sellers	Field sellers focused on 110; Inside proposal team had 150
NUMBER OF SELLERS	5	6
CLIENTS PER SELLER	Each seller originally had approximately 60 clients assigned to them	Ranged per seller from 8 up to 30
WIN RATE	35%	67%
AVERAGE MARGIN	9%	14%
SALES OVERALL	Inconsistent sales results per month, per quarter	Predicatable sales with 10 consecutive months of budget achievement and more accurate forecasts
GROWTH YOY	Limited YOY growth (had actually declined for 2 straight years)	Overall sales tripled
SELLERS EXCEEDING QUOTA	No seller exceeded their quota	4 out of 6
SELLERS NAMED TO PRESIDENTS CLUB	0 of 10 who can qualify	2 out of 10 who can qualify
RECOGNITION IN REGION	No regional recognition or team member recognition	Region earned most awards for 2 years at annual conference

Remember that critical distinction I mentioned. The rights worked to the highest achievement because everyone, including the executive team, was bought into what we were working to accomplish. It led to widespread success, but most of all widespread fun across the team.

"Less is more" is the best way to grow any business, large or small. It is achieved by knowing what best leads to your success as a company and demonstrating that commitment in all you do.

Chapter 11

POSITIONING THE RIGHT SOLUTION OFFERING
Matching Right Value with Need Rarely Loses

HAVE YOU EVER HAD TO FIX or repair something and then come to find that you bought the wrong-sized part? The part looks correct, but it simply does not fit exactly as it should. Because it is all you have to fix the issue, you work feverishly to make it fit. The net result is almost always the same: You either break the part while trying to make it work, or it does work, but only temporarily until that part that never fit in the first place ultimately breaks. When you are selling the products, services, and solutions within your portfolio of offerings, consider it no different than attempting to repair something. Each part either fits or it does not, and no matter how much you try to force the wrong parts to fit, you will most assuredly end up breaking something. More often than not, what is broken is a customer relationship you have worked to establish for a long time.

One point I want to make clear before I proceed further is that this chapter is based on the right solution and matching the right value for the customer. It is not based on the right product, the right service, the right software, or the right people. My approach to sales dictates that when I speak with customers, I am speaking about solutions and how those customers can and should receive value from the solution that I as a vendor provide. Why is that my view? First and foremost, I want my customer to know that what I offer is a solution to their needs, a solution to their concerns, and a solution for their business. I am the man with the solution. Additionally, it bothers me greatly that many vendors might have multiple capabilities within their portfolio of offerings for their customers, yet far too often sellers speak only about a single offering as opposed to other potential solutions that might be available to further enhance their need. This is especially limiting when the one and only offering being discussed is a low-margin product that could easily be offered with installation services and maintenance contracts. Yet time and time again, the discussion is about the product only.

Let's recall what I stated in "Chapter 4: Relationship Selling or Bust" about how to treat customers. It's about the customer, not about you as the seller. That said, the customer does not think about their vendor in terms of product sales only, services sales only, parts sales only, or consulting sales only. The customer thinks of their vendor as a provider of a service that supports all their business needs. Even when they need to purchase a product, the customer looks to the vendor to provide the service of product fulfillment that includes accepting the order on their behalf, ensuring that the product is delivered without a hitch, installing the product, and maintaining and supporting the product. Throughout that process, their seller should be the person who maintains a high level of communication with the customer to assure them that their order is underway and appropriate steps are being taken for successful delivery and handoff to the customer.

What I just described is what most every company provides their customers, which by definition is the fulfillment of a service that the company is offering. If customers looked at your company as a product-only fulfillment center, they would just order the lowest-priced product online, hope for the best in terms of the timing of the delivery, and not bother to speak with anyone beyond the day of the order. Stop limiting your own mind about the value you represent to your customer when you are the provider of an end-to-end service and solution. You bring tremendous value beyond just taking an order which the customer desires by the fact they are relying on you and not the internet.

There is no more important element to the selling and proposal process, in my view, than the level of quality and care you apply to what is being proposed and how we respond to the customer's needs. Specifically, you need to think about the right offering and the right focus and far less about a quick win. This is where I feel far too many deals are lost, leaving companies wondering what happened and who to blame. Will all deals fall under this discussion of right offering and right focus? Yes and no. Let me explain.

All companies must achieve certain initiatives in order to reach their goals. Often those initiatives might be achieved by positioning or selling a specific product over other supported products. Sellers and sales leaders often face similar requirements. But if I am speaking about right offerings, can that come in conflict with the goals of the company and its sellers? The answer is yes.

Here is a basic example in the area of technology: A customer needs to replace a router that has recently failed. Their needs related to functions are minimal, so nothing too feature-rich is needed—

just the basic routing functions will suffice. As a reseller for a manufacturer, you know the manufacturer offers a basic router that would satisfy the needs of the customer for, say, $3,000. The manufacturer also offers a more feature-rich model that costs $3,600. You and your company know that the more feature-rich model allows you, as the vendor, to receive a much higher margin on the product and after-sale rebates. In other words, if the vendor sells the basic model, they might earn a 5% margin; the more feature-rich version offers a 30% margin. Both the company and seller quotas are based on margin. What is the right choice?

Most companies will entice their sellers to sell the higher-margin product, and that seller will be placed in the situation of explaining to the customer why all those extra features the customer may have never thought they needed might one day be of value. The seller is now *acting* like a seller of product, not the individual working to be the relationship salesperson. The issue is real, and we all face it in product sales regularly.

Am I telling you to ignore your leadership and follow the right solution approach based purely on customer need? No. I have been in this situation as well, and realize that my model has to allow for the flexibility to know what is best for supporting the customer's needs while also meeting the company's strategic initiatives to grow profit. The challenge here is not an ethical one, either. The feature-rich model does provide everything the customer requires for their business to be successful, and likely does provide added value for future needs, even if unforeseen at the moment. As long as you explain to the customer the benefits of both products and they make their decision based on full disclosure of information, I see little concern that this could one day harm your relationship with them. You provided them all the options and they made their decision based on that information.

You did your job and supported both party's best interests in the end. That was the right solution. Had you not provided full transparency, I would feel differently.

Sellers and sales leaders also have to pay close attention to patterns of complacency or comfort zones when working with customers for a long period of time. This is not unusual, especially when doing business with customers with whom we have built long-standing relationships or what many may consider a simple product fulfillment-based relationship requiring nothing more than a price lookup and quick proposal. A request comes in as we have other things occurring at the same time, and the request is quickly processed to get the proposal out the door. Easy. These sound and feel like deals that are simple and do not take a high level of effort; just process them and get the PO out quickly. I agree that they should be simple, but I urge you not to overlook the importance of asking a few questions before just fulfilling them.

I fully agree with moving requests through the order and fulfillment process as quickly as is best for the customer. Earning money and earning it quickly for certain orders and customers is exactly what is best for all. But sometimes speed can lead us to overlook small details with big ramifications. That is where your relationship and designation as a valued partner has to play a role. You have to assist the customer in seeing what maybe they do not see as basic needs. Look at each request as unique, and have a natural desire as a seller to ask a few questions. You want the customer to be completely delighted with your efforts, not just the fulfillment of the order. Simple POs are nice, but overlooking an opportunity to prove your value as an innovative partner can have negative repercussions on your relationship. Always ask questions.

Let's more deeply discuss the differences and gray areas that can occur.

The Long-Term Relationship

In this first scenario, we should consider the customer that many of us are fortunate enough to have—a regular purchaser, with whom we have a trusting relationship. This situation is also the most dangerous, however, as it can allow our guard to drop. What happens in any relationship we develop, whether in business or in our personal lives? We get comfortable and begin to overlook the small things. We start to take the other person for granted, and this opens small gaps in the relationship. Those gaps allow competitors to enter the discussion, and then they turn into large cracks. Consider even what you hear from potential new customers who are thinking about leaving their existing vendors: "They only come in to collect the PO"? "We do not see them as often as we used to"? Is it even "They have not changed what they discuss with us and offer no innovation to help us grow—they just take our orders"?

The flaw of quickly processing a request to fulfill an order is that while it feels right for the customer because they needed it quickly, and for you as the seller because you made a quick sale and have more sales to make, it limits the potential for growth. It limits growth in the relationship, growth in the development in your awareness of customer needs or their awareness of new product offerings, and growth of the possibility for you as a seller to help the customer evolve to meet the ever-changing requirements of the marketplace and their own customers. You have become complacent—but you can change this pattern. In order to do so, you must face some necessary truths.

First, recognize that you never intended to become complacent with a customer. Your intention was to do your job well, find and develop good relationships with several key customers, possibly even build new friendships with those customers, and make a good living for yourself along the way. Unfortunately, along the way there also came demands from the company to grow your business in a short window of time, a quota that was likely larger than you expected, a manager who asks about pipeline growth and closed deals more regularly than you wish to answer the questions, and perhaps a spouse and family counting on your next commission to come in. Ultimately you develop into a seller who is always hurried and working feverishly to get to the next deal. But our business only does this if we allow it to. *If we allow it to.* This is a pattern you can change.

Am I recommending you initiate a deep discussion about every request? No. If you have a long-standing relationship with a customer, you should be familiar enough with their business to know the difference between a request that rectifies something that suddenly broke versus something that might be more significant over time. Let me give a quick example from my infrastructure background. A customer might request a sudden replacement of a ten-year-old router that just stopped working. They need to have it replaced quickly because a portion of the user population is unable to access the network. If you know their environment, you know that time is of the essence and replace the router without delay. You have already anticipated this failure anyway, due to the age of the router. The result: a satisfied customer.

But would asking several questions prior to making the order have hurt the sale? Maybe that was an opening to remind them about the plans you had discussed for their network in the next year or to mention how upgrading the router makes better sense based on their future plans.

What if the router is a new model installed only a year ago but has inexplicably stopped working? Would that raise a flag and require a broader discussion before just replacing to ensure that they are not overlooking a broader issue within the network? I hope so; this would also demonstrate your desire to become less a product seller and more a partner who provides a consultative-level benefit to the customer. It might not be just you having that discussion; you may include your technician as part of the review team. What matters in this discussion is not that you are selling, but that you are learning and offering knowledge and resources to assist the customer in better understanding why the failure occurred. I recognize that the immediacy of the need may dictate you put a new part right away; you do not want to linger during a network outage that could negatively impact the customer's business. But you can move quickly alongside consultative engagement as part of the service you offer. If the customer simply declines, make a note and save the discussion for a later time, but make sure you continue to offer your company's experience in helping them improve their business every chance you get. They will remember you have offered—just like they always remember when you do not.

The New Customer Relationship

Congratulations, you have a new customer! Take the time to celebrate your success. Okay, now your five minutes is up; get back to selling. You are officially in the honeymoon period with your new customer, that period of uncertainty when you want to assure the customer that everything you or any representative of your company does is done with excellence for fear of even slightly disappointing them. Along with satisfaction, this new sale also brings stress. It was a long road of selling and negotiating to get the customer to the point where they were now, ready to have you become their vendor of choice—or more accurately, their trusted advisor. You don't want anything to place the health and long-term success of this relationship at risk. The initial sale is only a small first step toward a bigger hill to climb if you are going to truly expand and strengthen this relationship.

There is no better time to begin formulating a plan to define how you and your team will mature the account over time. Many companies use an account plan model for this effort, and beginning this process early will add greater value to your success than finding reasons to delay the process. The account plan will be discussed in greater detail within the right strategic planning chapter of the book, so I will not repeat what is already provided, but I would be remiss if I did not mention the value of the plan here as well.

Since this is the right solution-offering chapter of the book, I remind you that your newly earned relationship must be built on trust and respect. You are the face of your company in the eyes of the customer, and while their decision to work with you is a vote of confidence that you are backed by a well-established and strong organization, they will hold you accountable for knowing not only your company business but also theirs. This takes on numerous responsibilities tied back to the practices shared in right strategic planning, right customer, right people, right culture, and even right funnel as you expand your presence within the customer. With all those rights, you will be the lens through which the company gets

> **You are the face of your company in the eyes of the customer ... they will hold you accountable for knowing not only your company business but also theirs.**

to know the details of the customer's aspirations and business expectations; ultimately, you will also be the voice of the customer when assuring that your company colleagues live up to the level of excellence you have promised. Whether proposal team members, technical personnel, administrative assistants, or even executives, you must ensure that all personnel your customer interacts with act according to these values and trust that they will say yes when it is right to do so and vice versa. Your team can be a great benefit, but the slightest error by one member can be an open invitation to the competition. Customers love when their world is made simpler, and it is up to you to ensure that your colleagues can work as a team to make that happen.

Identifying and Establishing New Prospective Customers

Trying to not only identify but open channels of communication with prospective customers who you hope could become your next top customer is like venturing into uncharted waters. You are essentially in blind date mode, and if you have ever been on a blind date, you know that moment you show up the judgment begins. In a date scenario, you are forced to wonder if they like how you dress, how you look, what you say or don't say—and what if they veer into talk of politics? Do you even go there? Could what you say close the door on your future relationship or the next date?

Unfortunately, it could. You truly have no idea what a customer might judge you on, and it may be more trivial than you can imagine. You must always be prepared and focused on the reason you are there. You don't need to be so focused that you lose your personality or act stiff, but do not allow yourself to let down your guard and risk getting blindsided. Recall what we stated throughout the book: The most important part of any new relationship for a customer is trust and respect. They come into a meeting looking to assess you: *Is this an individual I can trust to help me and my business? Do I respect the way they conduct themselves?* Hopefully, you'll conduct yourself well enough to begin a long-term relationship.

How do you establish trust and respect? Thankfully, I learned very early in my selling career the value of honesty and truth. I am not saying I refused to laugh at a customer's joke that I didn't really find funny; we all have to do what it takes to be social and keep conversation flowing. I simply learned early on how to say the two words sellers are most fearful of saying, and the reason most customers distrust sellers: *yes* and *no*.

A seller fears that saying no, even when no is the best option, will close the door on their sale and their potential for a future with that account. In turn, customers have a hard time trusting sellers because more often than not, they are not 100% confident that their seller really can accomplish what they promise when they say yes or that they are not saying yes when they should have said no. The truth will set you free—and not only that, but it will gain you greater access into that customer's business environment than you ever would have gained by yessing your way in.

Understand that customers today are under the same level of business and financial pressure as you. They risk their job with every chance they take on a new vendor they have never met. How are they supposed to know whether or not you are placing their livelihood at risk because you are not mature or ethical enough to say no? The best way to grow a relationship with a customer is to be transparent. Share with them how your offerings can best serve their needs and when it is not an exact match. Share with them where gaps in offerings to their stated needs may exist and offer up ideas on how they can better meet those needs. That is how a consultant-like relationship works, and it demonstrates very clearly for that prospective customer why you are the person they can trust and will respect. More positives occur in a truthful relationship than one forged by dishonest tactics.

If you doubt me, feel free to go say yes when you should have said no. See what anxiety you cause yourself and your company as you try to come up with a way to provide what you said you could do, or deal with triaging the issue after your product falls short of the customer's desired expectations. Fixing an issue is very difficult when it was not something your team ever specialized in to begin with and they do not know the best answers. Valuable time is lost in the triage process for the customer; in addition to being burdened because of the slow response time, sellers often explain the delay with lame excuses, worsening the relationship. Regardless of whether you are able to resolve the issue or not, trust has been broken and your road to a long-lasting relationship has taken a detour.

When sellers come to me with a new opportunity but want to provide a non-standard offer, they often tell me "This is the door opener to more business!"

My response will most assuredly be: "Keep in mind that doors also open into the alley—make sure you know the difference between the front door and the back door."

Your success will grow immeasurably by spending the time to position the right solution to fit the customer's needs.

Chapter 12

RIGHT RELATIONSHIPS ACCELERATE SUCCESS
Relationships Can Help Grow or Slow

IN SALES WE MUST FOCUS on building strong relationships with the most appropriate contacts within the customer to achieve our goals. That is what sales has become: a relationship-based process (as discussed more broadly in "Chapter 3: Relationship Selling or Bust"). But now that you understand why relationship selling matters, it is up to you, the seller and sales leader, to know how best to differentiate which relationships within a customer are more likely to help you grow your sales over time and which will impede your progress. Each play a role in your customer relationship, with some being decision makers, others who influence the decision, and still others whose relationship adds value in differing ways. The SPIN Methodology for selling provides several simple ways to identify the buyer by using such designations as focus of power (FOP), focus of receptivity (FOR), and focus of dissatisfaction (FOD), which can be useful designations.

As a note, I am a fan of using some form of sales methodology and have myself applied SPIN and Miller Heiman at past companies. These structures can provide great results when applied consistently across the business. I believe that the sales methodology that is best for you is the one that best fits your company-wide culture and sales structure. My personal view is that all methodologies have merit, and their approaches are actually quite similar. My primary recommendation is that if you plan to implement a sales methodology, train all employees who have any level of interaction with the customers and ensure they all use the methodology every day and in all that they do. If you are not going to apply it with vigor, consistency, and longevity, the variance will be such that it is not worth applying at all.

The real benefit of knowing your different buyer types, whether you use the SPIN acronyms or not, is that it makes a difference in how many opportunities you will win or lose, and how quickly. All relationships inside a customer business have some benefit but you need to know as early as possible the precise value of each role. If you don't make the effort to learn this, you could spend a significant amount of time working with the incorrect individuals while a much more significant opportunity passes you by. From day one of the relationship development process, it is relevant to know which customer contacts will sign POs, which will bury you in paperwork, and who is likely to burn up your time in endless discussions with no ability to approve or purchase what you sell. You will experience them all in nearly every customer you work with, so early identification will allow you to successfully maneuver through the maze of contacts time and time again.

Let me identify my own customer types by title for simplicity and better clarity.

TABLE 6: RELATIONSHIPS

TITLE	BENEFIT OF RELATIONSHIP
PROCUREMENT	A gatekeeper level responsible for working and managing relationships with vendors and running the PO/RFI/RFP/order process. They are good to speak with about product-related needs, but they can impede progress and are always tasked with pushing for discounts.
HUMAN RESOURCES	Supports procurement requests, but not highly engaged with vendors unless needed. Rarely are they an influencer or approver unless the engagement includes impact to personnel.
LEGAL OR CONTRACTS	Will work MSA and SOWs with procurement. Rarely an approver but will advise company if you are challenging to do business with.
MANAGER	They will speak with vendors and share scope needs, but often have limited ability to sign orders without a supervisor's approval. They can make recommendations, but can also waste time. Many sellers spend a lot of time here because they will talk and accept lunches, but they do not sign off on orders beyond a defined purchase price.
DIRECTOR	Slightly higher approval power than managers, but do provide more input in vendor selection. They will speak with the vendor as needed for projects. Have approval authority at defined purchase price. Work to understand their approval authority level.
VICE PRESIDENT OR SVP	Typically signature level on deals up to a specific value. Can also approve or recommend a vendor for a larger deal that requires executive approval. Gain input from Director and middle management.
EXECUTIVE TEAM (C-LEVEL)	Top most approver in the company, but traditionally involved in only the largest purchases. They take recommendations directly from the VP or SVP level, who conduct most of the due diligence on vendor selection.

The examples may vary slightly between customers, as companies can differ based on their size and organizational structure. However, the roles identified within Table 6 align closely to roles most often found in the enterprise- and large commercial-based customers.

The customer environment has changed significantly in the past 20 years, and it has become ever more challenging for a seller to penetrate new customers due to numerous layers of bureaucracy and gatekeeping mechanisms. To this end, partners and friends can be a valuable asset for supporting your efforts to gain access to a new customer relationship. Regardless of how you get access to that customer contact, learn how the layers of the organization work for all deals within the customer, whether for products or services.

Let me demystify immediately a common myth in sales: the crazy notion that all sellers need to be speaking with the C level to get a sale. Be realistic! You are not going to be speaking with the C level, at least not with the majority of customers. With the exception of very small companies, the C level is rarely engaged in the selling process; they will almost never be engaged in traditional procurement at a Fortune 500 company unless the opportunity is of substantial value. Could they be signing the proposal or contract for a new vendor? Maybe, but certainly not in every situation. And even if they sign, it does not mean they will take the time to meet every seller who supports their business, nor do they want the seller to call them directly. If your executives are waiting to speak with their C levels, they will have to get over it in most situations until the time is right or if at all.

Customers have authority levels predefined for signing off on deals or contracts. You can learn that structure very quickly by asking the right questions, and a seller or sales leader should know the authority chain at a customer every time a new deal is waiting to be finalized.

A seller needs to focus their energy to learn who within the company approves or signs for specific types of new business. Even the signing authorities more often than not gain their information from a lower-level authority who is responsible for vendor research and selection. The signing authority is not necessarily engaged; they just sign when their direct report provides their assessment.

It is common for a seller to ask their customer about the approval process. The customers know it sets good expectations and enables for more efficient engagement on deals. Take note that when a customer does define the hierarchy they also want you to know to follow it. Customer relationships can quickly dissolve if they feel you are going around them in the process or directly to their superior without approval. This is also valuable information for you as a seller to have when your own executives are asking questions related to the deal. Your knowledge of the authority and signature chain of personnel will demonstrate your depth of awareness about the customer.

Some basic questions to ask might be:

- As my primary contact, are you also the approver of the opportunity and the individual responsible for signing?
- If someone else signs, do they also get involved in the review process?
- Are you the individual who has the final say on endorsing a vendor?
- Who is the signing authority? Do they work in this office location or another?
- Will there be opportunity for both companies' executive teams to meet one another? If so, when would that normally occur?
- Will I be working primarily with you or will I also need to work with your boss throughout the process?

- For each individual role within the organization, what is the policy on who signs and what are the defined dollar values each are able to approve and sign?

The above examples reflect some of the questions that can help you define the authority levels at your customer—but again, every company varies. Ask the questions of every customer so you know precisely what you should expect during active deals. Just make sure they understand that your need to know is based on setting proper expectations within your company, not so you can make random calls to the higher-level individuals to introduce yourself. Most customers will be reluctant to share the names of their peers or executives unless they have that proper level of trust in you as a seller.

The most important thing during the relationship development process is to understand the difference between customer contacts that make things happen and contacts that have no problem enjoying a free meal but have little ability to make a decision or sign off on a deal. Identify each early, spend your time wisely, and maximize your success.

Chapter 13

GET YOUR SALES FUNNEL RIGHT
Right Opportunities Matter for Best Success

THIS SECTION FOCUSES ON the value of quality within a sales or pipeline. To be clear, let me repeat the most important word: **quality.** I do not focus merely on a quantity of deals. While I have been in sales for many years and have worked at all levels of the selling organization, I am continually amazed at how so many are still tasked with building a pipeline based primarily on quantity rather than quality. I believe much of this has to do with the belief so many sales personnel have in the old adage that if you throw enough things against a wall something will stick. But this approach to pipeline development is enormously flawed and will cost you more time, sales and money than it will gain you.

Not everyone is to blame for this misconception. Let's face it: if a sales leader tells a seller to build a pipeline that is three times their quota or else, the seller is going to put anything they can into the pipeline to make the funnel appear to look full. This is especially true if they know that once they increase the pipeline value to triple the value of the quota, the sales leader will stop harassing them. And yes, it can often feel like harassment to a seller. We all know the way some sales leaders position their management style.

But now that the funnel is full, the sales and commissions should start rolling in, right? More often than not, this is the furthest from reality. While it may appear full, the opportunities you have entered may be of lesser quality when you pull back the curtain and inspect them more closely. In Table 7, let's take an example of 100 opportunities entered in a seller funnel and break them down from a quality viewpoint.

TABLE 7: FUNNEL

NUMBER OF OPPORTUNITIES	% OF OVERALL FUNNEL	TYPE OF OPPORTUNITY
5 to 10	10%	Opportunities identified as having the highest level of potential for closing as a won deal.
10 to 20	20%	Opportunities are needs you know the customer has discussed as business issues, and with the proper time and effort they might turn into a priority, requiring the customer to purchase. Keep them on the "watch" list.
20 to 40	40%	Opportunities have not been stated as needs; rather, they are activities where you are attempting to create interest. But the sales leader was pushing you for pipeline growth, so you entered them—not as activity-based, but as true pipeline opportunities with actual dollar values.
Remaining 30 or more	30%	What I will refer to as "pipeline gap fillers." Not real opportunities and not yet activity you are discussing with a customer; more like future activity that can fill the rest of the 3x funnel gap and stop the sales leader from questioning you daily on your pipeline.

While they may not be exact to every pipeline, do these percentages remind you of what makes up your funnel? Is it slightly easier to distinguish why a funnel with triple the leads may really only be generating a fraction of that in true potential for success? I am asking sales leaders to question this long-standing traditional thinking around funnel creation; it is not the true personal formula for success.

Think about it: If every sales leader at every company throughout every industry with an active sales force uses the three-times-your-quota method of funnel creation, wouldn't it make sense for that to be the most widely successful method to grow a funnel? After all, it would be without a doubt the most widely adopted. Why else would so many business leaders use this approach if it does not work every time?

The answer is not that hard to understand. It was most likely developed in the early history of sales as a good standard for a salesperson who had a single product to sell and literally no competition in the marketplace. If 33% of their customers on average bought their product, their pipeline would need to be three times their quota to be successful. It was a simple mathematical factor for all to use, and easy to predict and measure for both sales leader and seller alike. And for a time, it worked just fine—but it's just not effective thinking today. You need to be more prescriptive than that in our much more competitive and complex marketplace.

As I have discussed throughout this book, the marketplace has evolved considerably over many years. Customers' businesses are continually faced with increased demands to grow revenue yet reduce costs, all while creating new and innovative offerings in what have now become very complex environments. Simultaneously, competition in the market has grown dramatically, and nearly all goods and services are faced with the same challenges of being so commoditized that little profit can be earned. Years ago, that salesman with a single product offering I mentioned above had little if any competition to compete against; today, he might have dozens, if not hundreds, of competitors all vying for the PO that a customer plans to award to a single provider. That makes every sales engagement intense and forces you as a provider to quickly consider what would normally be considered unusual acts, such as cutting your price, which impacts your margin, while also trying to increase the value of the deal you hope will overcome the next nearest competitor's offer. Increased value normally just means that your company is providing something extra for little or no additional price increase. But using these tools, you forge ahead, fight the good fight, and win...or do you?

You were selected the provider of choice and your company just announced your new business as the win of the week, so it certainly appears you did win! Congratulations! But wait—what do you mean, your commission was half what you thought due to reduced margins? Not to mention you've just realized that you lost one of the other top opportunities you were counting on while you were trying to provide your sales leaders daily/weekly pipeline updates, trying to speak to all 100 pipeline customers as quickly as possible for status updates, and update your entries in your CRM. You seem very busy, and with the 3x funnel you created, that must mean you are destined for financial success. Yet your success is short-lived. The reality is that you have built a fragile foundation for your funnel, which resulted—as it has for so many—in less-than-favorable results both short and long term.

Let me help you consider a better approach that applies to all levels of a selling organization, not just field sellers or sales leaders. I believe that this is the way every organization has to adapt to the evolving marketplace if best outcomes are truly desired. Obviously, each and every business must modify some elements of the method to align best with their business and or product category, but the concept remains the same.

Just like I have stated in previous chapters related to the right strategy, the right leaders, the right people, and the right customers, it is incredibly important to also focus your attention, time, and efforts on the right opportunities. When you do not, you allow other factors to risk your most important opportunities' place in the win column. I am not insensitive to the fact that we all have a responsibility to the company we work for and are required to properly develop a funnel that best represents an opportunity for our company and its employees to properly project short and long-term sales success. However, I am recommending that as sales professionals, we need to better articulate and take action on those methods that will allow the company to reach their maximum potential while helping ourselves individually reach ours. This is easy to say, of course, yet reality will tell you that it is easier to gain commitment to this approach from the leadership team when it has proven successful. Without results, the old methods and thinking will not go away overnight.

Keep in mind that the company you work for is trying to sell a specific type of product or service. In many ways, it is a stated or defined offer. As sales professionals, you have to fully embrace what differentiates your offering from that of the competition, and what will help differentiate your offerings to the customer as the most effective for achieving their business objectives. You must do all this while understanding what limitations exist in the offering to ensure that you are selling something your company can live up to. I am using the word "embrace" intentionally in this section. All too often, we want our offerings to be all things to all customers. Be honest: They are not, and it is not your company's responsibility to make it seem that way by providing products with unlimited features and specifications. If products and services did have unlimited capabilities, then sellers would really not be needed; the products could sell themselves. This is why selecting the right customers with the right opportunities while proposing the right offerings make the best sense.

> **If products and services did have unlimited capabilities, then sellers would really not be needed; the products could sell themselves.**

Differentiation is what separates the competition, and it is beneficial for both provider and customer in a competitive marketplace. Maybe there are key attributes your offerings provide that differentiate them from the competition; maybe it is the people and resources your business has to support the customer; maybe it is just low price. Regardless of what that intangible is, you need to know clearly what makes your offering stand out and why that customer should realistically select you. More importantly, you have to be realistic in how you assess the customer's needs and fully understand the difference between an opportunity you can win wholly and one that might seem like a win but that will later lead to unfulfilled needs and customer dissatisfaction.

Never lose sight of the fact that in most scenarios, the customer desires require a provider to alleviate a pain they are feeling in their business, and they are looking to you to make it go away as painlessly as possible. The truth hurts when you have a quota over your head during this assessment of the deal, but it's better that you tell yourself the truth now as opposed to spending countless hours and resources chasing an opportunity you knew you were not well positioned to win just because it was large and would make a quota impact.

Worst of all, as experience has shown, the losses tend to be compounded as you begin to also lose other "better" opportunities within your funnel due to the inordinate amount of time spent working on the wrong opportunities. Opportunities take time to move through the sales cycle, regardless of whether in the end you win or you lose. You have to consider the time and effort you lose supporting other key engagements when a single opportunity consumes most of your energy. Is this deal worth it? Or are you risking the best deals within your funnel for an opportunity that is too high risk to spend valuable time on? No, you cannot spread your time across all your opportunities effectively enough to win them all. More often than not, when you spread your energy across many, you simply lose them all. When you focus your time and effort on a select few, you are better positioned to win more and earn more with a higher level of focus and quality.

What matters first and foremost in the pipeline-to-success ratio for me is the quality of the deals you place in your funnel. Consider some version of the following questions to decide whether or not a deal is worth pursuing.

Do I fully understand what the customer is looking to solve? If not, ask more clarifying questions related to business impact and scope.

Does my portfolio of offerings address the customer requirements? If so, does it address them in full or just portions of them? Which portions matter most to your company's ability to delivery successfully?

If your offering only provides part of the solution they desire, openly ask **the importance of receiving the full solution from a single provider**. If the offer lacks certain features, how much weight will that carry in the customer's decision process? What value does each feature hold in the decision?

Am I currently doing business with this customer as an incumbent provider, or would this be my first opportunity? The importance of this question will directly relate to level of risk a customer might take. If customer is working with you for the first time, they are more likely to try you in a smaller, less risky opportunity than they would in a significant business-impacting way. Know the difference and how it impacts that customer.

How strong is my relationship with this customer? Is it deep enough that I will be recognized as a trusted and respected provider?

Is my relationship with the individual making the decision and resulting in past or current success? If not, what would it take to make that occur?

Is the relationship I have someone with who strongly endorses me and is a decision maker or influencer in the decision process?

How is the competition seen within this customer? Are they an incumbent provider? Are they known to have a strong relationship with key stakeholders and decision makers?

In an incumbent situation, it is very important to clearly understand the **customer's level of frustration that is leading them to change providers.** Customers will often vent their frustration and tell competitors that they want to change from an incumbent provider, but the reality is that nearly 90% of the time customers stay with the incumbent due to the strength of their relationship, a fear of change, transition of service concerns, or the single biggest factor—the incumbent provided a cost reduction.

Are they maintaining consistent communications with me demonstrating a desire to work with me as a partner?

If this is an RFP process, how many vendors are they allowing to respond? Did your company assist with the development of the RFP or did another incumbent provider assist? Both questions can provide insight in the realistic ability for your company to be awarded the business or if you are just being allowed to respond to meet a minimum quota for vendor respondents.

Will they require a reference account? Do we have one that meets their criteria?

What else will matter to that customer in a positive or negative way? Again, be honest.

When assessing opportunities with these questions, it is always best to remove the concern or emotion related to your quota. That kind of fear will only lead you to make incorrect choices. While I know you have financial obligations, this is often the very thing that blinds you from being honest with yourself.

I also believe that a good way of identifying and qualifying what you should or should not add to your pipeline is proactively thinking ahead in the selling cycle and considering what it takes to win those deals. Do not only brainstorm things you might be good at selling to those customers later on, but go right to assessing whether they are deals in which you believe the customer would select your company as the provider. For this part of the qualification process, consider the steps you normally take later in the selling process. When working on target accounts, I often use not only account reviews but win plans for specific key deals. A tool I personally utilize within a win plan for visually showing the results of a win assessment is the SPIN Vulnerability Analysis, which is part of the SPIN methodology as shown in Chart 1 below.

CHART 1: SPIN VULNERABILITY ANALYSIS

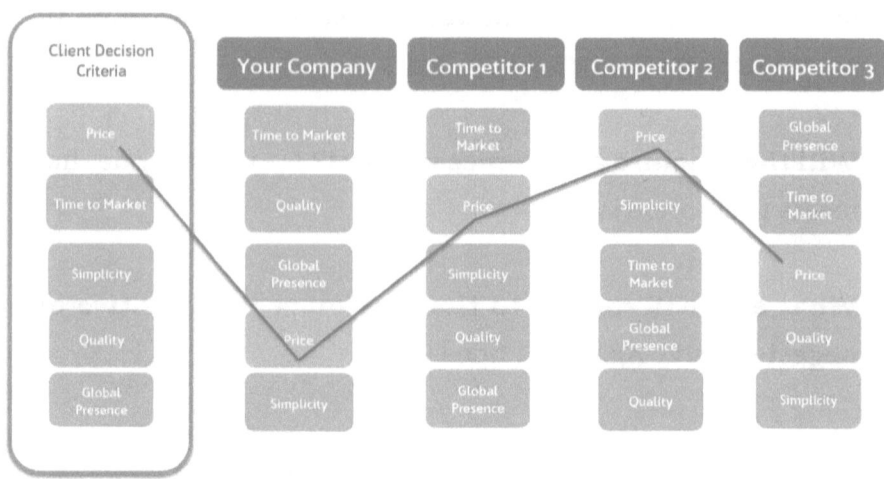

The focus SPIN applies within the Vulnerability Analysis is specific to the customer decision-making criteria during the selection process. When properly and honestly applied, this tool visually identifies known comparisons that would need to be overcome to better improve the odds of selling and winning a given opportunity. This is somewhat like a stack ranking that customers apply to you and your competitors. Your ability to be recognized as the top provider is your ability to best align with their most relevant business needs. More importantly, this analysis identifies whether the gaps in your ability to win are so great that it makes more sense to simply not continue in the engagement process.

If you assess that an opportunity is not a proper fit, disengage early. It is far less costly to your business and the customer relationship to make that choice or even lose early than to come in second place. If and when you do decide to not support an opportunity, have a plan in place on how best to discuss your decision with the customer. The more effort you put into crafting your message and clearly and concisely articulating the reasons, the better it demonstrates to the customer your level of professionalism.

While this often feels like a very difficult discussion to have with your customers, they will respect you for not placing their business or careers at risk just to try to make a commission. The key is to inform them early in the process, before they spend too much time counting on you to provide something that you might be unable to support. Doing so will prove to them your level of commitment as a true partner to their business and the success of the relationship. This approach will lead to far greater potential for business from that customer than forcing something that was not a good fit and living with customer satisfaction issues from that day forward.

Chapter 14

THE RIGHT QUOTA OR BUDGET
Accelerators or Inhibitors?

THERE IS A WELL-KNOWN QUOTE that in my view perfectly frames the concept of this chapter: "The definition of insanity is doing the same thing over and over again and expecting different results." The quote is attributed to Albert Einstein, primarily because people have attributed the quote to him over and over again over the last century. That must make it correct, right? As it turns out, no; the quote has also been attributed to Mark Twain, Benjamin Franklin, or possibly the Chinese proverbs. Yet we continue as a society to believe it was said by Einstein; after all, the quote was clearly made by an intelligent person, and many of the intelligent people we know seem to assume it was him.

You will see that I have devoted more pages to this chapter than any other within the book. That is not because I consider it the most important right of your success—though it is an essential piece—

but more so because I have seen firsthand over my career a lack of respect the budget or quota have as a differentiator in reaching unlimited success. Far too many times, I have seen budget creation as the simple act of defining a number to be allocated, not a true vision or strategy about how that number could accelerate your potential for success.

To express this more succinctly, too many executives start the year by creating an annual budget first. Only after that is defined do they begin developing a business strategy to achieve that number. What I am stating in this chapter is that had the strategy come first, it is highly possible that the company-wide budget may have been defined differently, even higher, due to the predefined number not dictating the minimum level of success needing to be achieved. Because when a budget is defined first, the strategy is built on minimum achievement, not greatest potential.

Let me state before I begin that for the purposes of this chapter I will only use the term "quota," specific to the individual sellers' financial expectation and "budget" is more specific to the sales leadership team-wide obligation or the company as a whole. As a seller or sales leader, you understand that different companies may refer to either your individual quota or your team-wide designated budget.

> *When a budget is defined first, the strategy is built on minimum achievement, not greatest potential.*

It's time to step beyond the mentality that your business as a company needs to grow a standard 3-5% per year. For years this has been the definition of insanity, as the quote would intend. Read on for a thought-provoking discussion of what a quota can be and how rethinking it can benefit your business. I hope to make you think more broadly.

Which Comes First: Quota or Strategy?

All companies have a strategy for their overall business success; without one, the company and its employees would just wander aimlessly. That said, when executives speak with a sales leader, is their very first question to that leader "What is the quota you assigned to your sellers this year?" or "What is your sales strategy and direction for the team this year?" We know it would be the latter. In fact, I will go so far as to say if you as a sales leader approach an executive and tell them you assigned quotas across your team, they will normally respond by asking how you plan to achieve it, rather than just saying "good work." Why? Because the most important thing to executives and leadership is how each business unit and individual seller plans to attain their defined goals—not the actual goals themselves. You are welcome to prove me wrong by asking an executive the question, but I am confident they will answer that they think about overall strategy and plan is paramount.

So why, at the beginning of every new fiscal year, are sales leaders often presented a predefined growth number and told to create a plan to hit the number prior to receiving the companywide strategic plan? If we are really interested in the overall plan, shouldn't they be asked to create the strategy so that they can then determine what the potential for the growth number should be? This calls into question whether the business' annual success model is a strategy for achieving the minimum budget or a budget for maximizing the strategy. From my experience and many interactions with other leaders and executives, it is more often a strategy to achieve the minimum budget that was initially, often without careful thought, assigned first. When you take that approach, you receive only minimum outcomes to achieve that budget only.

This seems like such limited thinking from executives who are likely the most strategic thinkers in the company. Budgets represent such an important part of growth potential, yet little to no thought is given to the strategy behind them prior to setting the growth number. Listen, executives: by defining a number prior to a strategy, you never truly uncover the unlimited potential beyond the number. In essence, you are building your plans to reach minimal success, as sellers and sales leaders believe that 100% is the end goal. That cannot be the best outcome, when what we really desire in business is for all people to be performing toward and achieving their limitless potential. Had the strategy been set first, with team members all defining the business they might sell, broken down by offerings and specific customers, their projected outcomes may have been much higher than had the quota been assigned first.

> **What we really desire in business is for all people to be performing toward and achieving their limitless potential.**

Consider an example. The overall companywide budget number that was defined prior to creating a strategy was $100 million. This assumes a 5% growth target year over year. You would be successful by achieving 100% of that number. But what if the team strategized prior to creating a number for the fiscal year, and that review led to the belief that the business could reasonably achieve $120 million and identified areas of potential growth that would not have been found otherwise? The new number shows a potential for 20% more revenue. Yet with a number defined prior to strategy, sellers could take their foot off the gas if their compensation plans demonstrated no true benefit of going beyond $100 million or 100% attainment. They could hold on to the other 20% for the following fiscal year, when they will personally need it most depending on their compensation plan structure. Especially true for companies that do not build overachievement payout in their plans.

Motivation

Let me start by clarifying that while all companies allocate sellers individual quotas, it is not the truest motivator of higher sales, as leadership would like to believe. It is an intimidator, maybe, but not a motivator. It sounds good for a leader to call it a motivator during pipeline reviews, and while it is believed that quotas may influence sellers to work harder, let's stop confusing intimidating someone with motivating someone. A motivated person takes action at their own volition with a sense of purpose, passion, commitment, and a high desire to succeed. The right strategy, right leadership and right offering can generate this increased level of enthusiasm. An individual being intimidated is for the most part doing the opposite; they are likely uncommitted to the task, lacking belief and passion in their potential for success, and more often than not doing it simply because they are being pushed by leadership and being led to believe their job might be at risk. Which of the two do you think generates greater results? Which situation would motivate you personally to achieve at higher levels?

Sales purists reading this may say that everyone needs motivation to help them reach just a little higher than they would have without it. This is why football coaches scream at subpar players, grab their facemasks, and force them to practice drills more than others…so they can reach their true potential, right? Yet those football players that never reach the coaches' desired potential sit on the bench during games and only get used when necessary. They did likely reach their true potential—just enough to wear the uniform and get a participation trophy.

Why? It's all up to them. Even the most skilled individual will never reach their potential if they are not mentally in the game or internally motivated to achieve higher success, regardless of how much we yell, push, and motivate. The unmotivated player simply ends up on the junior team or benched, no matter what the coach does to motivate them. In sales, there is no junior team or participation trophy. The seller is always on the varsity team, always in the limelight, and always expected to reach their true potential on every sale, or they risk being cut from the team.

Think back to the chapters on the right strategy, right people, and right leaders. When you have all of these properly established, you need not motivate. The right people will drive you more than you drive them. By then you simply have to be a good leader and lead the strategic direction of the business with confidence. As a leader, you just need to stay the course of the strategy and keep distractions away. If a seller has to be motivated and does not have the innate sense of urgency or passion to sell more every day, you likely have the wrong person, not the wrong quota. Unless, of course, leadership has allocated such an unattainable quota that it is limited by what you offer as a company, sales cycles, delivery models, or other factors. In this situation, your quota has actually demotivated people from doing what they aspire to do. Now you not only miss attaining the number, but you will see the right people being motivated to leave the company. Studies have concluded that, on average, 55% of sellers will attain their assigned quota and 45% will not. Naturally motivated sellers will more regularly be in that 55% on their own; few will need your motivation. Most will just need you to lead and support their efforts. Neither you nor a number should get in their way.

Consider a basic success formula for most in sales leadership roles:

(SELLER + QUOTA) X SALES = EARNINGS

Does this type of formula-based thinking look familiar to you as a sales leader or seller? For the traditional sales leader, the thinking is that a seller with a quota will be driven to achieve sales, and by doing so, will earn a commission for themselves. After all, you cannot argue that a seller wants to be paid when the sale is complete, as the formula indicates. So if you agree with the formula, then are the sellers motivated by the potential for the sale, the potential for the earnings from the sale, or the calculation you created to build the quota you allocated to them? I am confident the calculation is not what motivates the best sellers and, in fact, inhibits your overall success. The inclusion of quota within the formula is your breaking point. It is not the motivator you want it to be but can be the factor that limits theirs and the company's potential.

The only rational argument you can have for me is that the formula for a seller to achieve success should have read:

(RIGHT STRATEGY + RIGHT PEOPLE) X
(RIGHT CUSTOMERS + RIGHT OFFERINGS) = SALES

When you hire a seller who is naturally motivated to begin with, support them with a well-defined business strategy that motivates them further and allow them to do what they like to do the most and are best at your best outcomes are the result. In this situation, selling will occur at a higher rate of outcome regardless of the quota you assign.

Consider as well when running your business based on the formula *(Right Strategy + Right People) x (Right Customers + Right Offerings) = Sales*, which has nothing to do with financial calculations, that you will not be limiting the potential of individual sellers or the team as a whole, just creating revenue. My experience in sales leadership and operations has consistently shown me the one thing that always holds true for attaining goals is a well-defined strategy led and followed by the leadership and people they lead. Achieve and retain the proper level of customer and employee satisfaction and success will be unlimited. Please note that nowhere within this paragraph did I say a well-structured calculation. I did not even say quota. True salespeople do not need a quota or financial expectation hanging over their head in order to reach their highest potential or achievements. Your best sellers are highly competitive, success-oriented, desire to be recognized as the best at what they do, and most importantly, want unlimited potential to earn. Not unlike top athletes, their internal passion drives them to reach higher to achieve success, not the milestone.

We tend to overthink the traditional creation process of a seller quota calculation because it is important to the business leaders to demonstrate they reach specific financial expectations. After all, you can't sell or earn the largest potential for growth if boundaries exist in your path. In other words, you have very smart people working hard to show their intelligence in the quota calculation process, which is actually curtailing the true potential of the business. It's the point where intelligence creates risk and you miss that extra 20% of potential shown earlier. We get in our own way of being great. If you want success, short and long term, then hire the right leadership to craft the right strategy for the business, including a well-defined vision, business strategy, marketing strategy, sales GTM, customer engagement model, delivery model, and P&L. Once that is complete and you trust that you have all the core elements defined, ensure you have the right leaders in sales to provide the proper leadership to the plan and hire the right people to bring in the opportunities. It is that vision and strategy, along with the right leaders to implement it, that will maximize the right sellers to perform at their best. It's not a calculation or quota, which is by its nature a limiting factor for many company's outcomes. This moves the main motivator from being the quota to the sales leadership and the seller. I will always place my bet on the right people over calculation.

In summary, focus on strategy, leadership, people and solutions first. Once those are established, consider the true potential of those elements in creating your team budget or sellers' quota. Establishing a predefined financial value before a plan will only limit the success you might have reached as sellers, sales leaders, and as a company.

Quotas Do Matter

Compensation models are a way of life for sales-based organizations, and all sellers know the company they work for must have models and plans that can impact their earnings potential. Let's face it: one of the most important elements of the compensation plan to the seller is the quota they know will be allocated to them. Not because it is their motivator for success, but because they must ensure it will not limit their ability to earn and achieve success. In fact, a smart seller asks about compensation and quota during the interview process before ever accepting a new role. Why? Because it matters to them how a potential employer thinks about the creation of both.

From the employer perspective, they should be interviewing to hire a seller, hopefully someone dynamic who can take their business to new heights. Or are they? Could it be they look very little at future potential and are just interviewing to see if they are good enough to fill the predefined gap in quota left behind by either the other individual who left or the new quota waiting to be allocated? Quotas are subjective, and often are more about leaders justifying that a financial goal has been set rather than truly defining what leads to greater outcomes. For many sales leaders, the method of quota setting is simple: What is the highest amount I can allocate to any one individual to achieve the desired outcome while also fulfilling my overall team budget obligation? This alone is often the barometer for how most sales leaders allocate a number to each person, as opposed to a true mathematical or analytical synopsis. Their reasoning might as well be "because I said so."

Sales leaders, you know when you're recruiting a new seller, the question of quotas will eventually come up. That seller will ask about average quota size, how it is calculated, how will they be paid, and earning potential, among numerous other questions. Knowing this, how well do you answer the question? Think about it. Do you answer using the three C's—concise, with clarity, and with confidence—or do you dance around the question or provide responses that do not state exactly what other sellers have done or how it is used to measure their success? If you dread the question, then you know the quota management process you have is flawed and of little value for retaining the right people long term. Your gut answers the question for you. You might as well stop the interview there and not hire the right people, since you already seem to know that your quota methods will likely limit their true potential and long-term retention.

As we continue this discussion, I will demonstrate that a quota matters greatly for sellers and sales leaders, but not one established in the traditional way. It must be calculated in a way that will enable your success, not inhibit your potential for success.

Quota Philosophy

Have sales leaders and executives ever actually stepped back to ask themselves why they are creating a quota? Does it truly drive seller outcomes, or does company after company in every industry use quotas simply because it's standard practice? *The allocation of a quota is what companies have always done throughout my selling career, so it must be right.* Did you ever check if your quota approach impeded success?

I am asking that we stop thinking traditionally. We have to consider all parts of the sales success scenario for a selling role. In my view, many sales leaders are limited in the ways they have to motivate sellers to aspire to be the best and sell more. Or, to be more fair, they have not been accustomed to being required to think in other ways beyond the quota and what they sell. Lauding the importance of the quota and measurement against it can actually hide the fact that many sales leaders and executives just do not consider more deeply the importance of being better coaches, trainers, mentors, and sales leaders. For some, this could be due to limited resources or poor leadership skills. Driving objectives and goals for success other than a financial time bomb—in the form of a poorly defined quota that goes off for a seller when the clock runs down to zero—is often an afterthought. My experience has shown that far too often the quota and compensation plan tends to become the sales leader and the measurement for everything that seller does, more so than the direction of their sales leadership. If the quota dictates how the seller will drive sales, then what purpose does the sales leader serve?

Why do quotas exist for a sales person?
- The company benefits from the ability to measure a seller's performance, not only against others on the team and across

the company, to motivate them and measure their performance in terms of employment.

- To apply proper expectation setting for the seller so they clearly understand the minimum goal their role needs to meet from a financial perspective.
- This process also draws a clear line from a predefined variable to how an employee in this role earns their level of payout. Most organizations have a seller compensation model that supports a guaranteed monthly base pay element as well as the commission earned as the variable pay portion of the compensation plan. The balance of pay between both differs based on company, but the method affords a company to gain the skill they desire but only pay for performance against that quota.
- The company is assured their annual financial obligation is fully allocated across business units and its team members.

More reasons exist, but these are the heart and soul of why most companies justify using quotas. I am not here to debate the philosophical benefits of having or not having a quota. I will provide rationale later why quotas are not necessary at all, but from a company perspective, I understand the need to measure sellers with a quota element. I am simply moving toward the idea that how we think about quotas is flawed and leading to lost potential. We need to move forward, past minimum success, to a true desire to reach goals well beyond a defined growth number.

That said, a quota should not exist simply because history has dictated this is how we do business or because a business leader lacks the capabilities or proper strategy to be more successful. Quota can be a useful mechanism for performance measurement, goal setting, and financial remuneration, but makes for a poor motivator and leader.

Rethinking a Traditional Approach

To best reset our thinking on how to create an individual seller quota, let's begin the discussion of quota allocation at $0.00. It will be easier to start a new approach from the ground up than to start from where your team's highest quota is allocated today and work in reverse.

Let's discuss why $0.00 as a quota makes more money for both seller and company in most situations. When a quota is defined for $5M, it does certainly show the seller what is financially expected of them by the company. More often than not, it is met with pushback and reasons why it is unattainable in an effort to gain a more favorable (smaller) quota. Some of these reasons might be legitimate and justified, while others are simply being designed to lower the quota and potentially increase earnings depending on how the compensation plan was designed. Regardless of the reason, these arguments are time spent not selling, and selling is what is most important in sales.

The $5M is also a stretch goal, which means it is designed as a means to motivate sellers to achieve their true potential. Not unlike the football player. Far too many will not. In fact, as I mentioned earlier, across any selling organization in any industry only 55% of the sales force will attain their quota for the fiscal year. This metric would lead you to assume that with only half the sales force reaching their goal, the fiscal year attainment for the overall company would fall short—yet oftentimes it does not.

What if mathematically the results show that instead of the company reaching 101% of their annual budget, they could have been reaching 110%, 120%, or more? 45% of the employees do not attain their quotas, but we often assume that means the 45% was a slight miss, when in fact those sellers who fell short may only have achieved 20% or less of their quota expectation. We also assume that the 55%

who achieved their quotas were those with the largest quotas across the team, rather than the smallest. Those must be the best sellers; the company must have met their annual budget due to the 55% being the highest quotas.

These two assumptions, while possibly still leading the company as a whole to their defined annual goals, may have actually missed the bigger issue that a significant amount of financial opportunity was missed due to a poorly defined quota allocation. In most organizations, they are simply counting on the law of averages and the proper balance of fear among their sellers to work out. I am not discounting personal motivation or sales skills in this scenario, but recognize that in a quota-focused environment, the management belief is all too often that quota drives behavior and outcomes, rather than the skilled employee and the leadership. This implies that a level of fear is required to get the point across. Yet fear has no benefit when quotas are often incorrectly allocated amongst the team of sellers to begin with, so those sellers with favorable quotas have little fear and those with incorrectly aligned quotas have only frustration.

What if a seller does not attain their quota? Are they considered a poor seller, or does it depend on the how far under the quota they achieved? The problem must not be a failure in the quota, many leaders reason, so it has to be the seller or sales leader. However, there are many other reasons that 45% do not hit their number.

Let me share a few common reasons sellers have given me for missing their quota:
- Not enough qualified leads
- Salespeople lack skills or training from time of hiring
- Company lacks proper offerings
- No formal sales process in place
- Sales leaders can't effectively coach reps or lead

- Process of ramping up sellers is too slow
- No decision from customer (need went away)
- Competition beating seller's company on price
- Sales burdened with administrative tasks
- Sellers assigned unrealistic quotes
- Deals not closed, but still in pipeline
- Salespeople lack skills from time of hiring

I am sure each reason has some level of merit in this discussion and that each has cost a seller a sale at some point within their selling career. And this list only represents a small sample of the reasons that might occur—all focused on why the company failed in the selling effort, not the seller.

Let's include those reasons that the seller simply has to own the responsibility for:

- Seller simply did not perform or focus on engagement
- Seller did not take the time to understand their offerings
- Seller was unable to establish the proper relationships with customers at multiple levels within organization
- Seller was unable to properly define the value of their offering to that of the competition
- Seller did not properly identify the need of the customer
- Seller does not have the selling skills that align with the solution or selling model
- Seller was not an effective hunter of new business, which the role required

These are real reasons too, and are examples of why it's so important to properly match right people with the right company to begin with. But there is still one component to the problem, one that even the right strategy and right leadership are all too often not immune to. All the best rights in a company can come to a screeching halt if the companywide budget for annual growth does not match reasonable expectations alongside the strategy. You know, the strategy that did not exist when the budget was set. This one element of the company can greatly alter the way final quotas are created and allocated and can ultimately place your sellers' and sales leaders' success, and thus that of the company, at risk. Building a strategy first is the single best way to avoid this risk.

Consider the amount of time, our most precious resource, spent on quota calculation. I myself have spent thousands of hours thinking about quotas, calculating factored and weighted systems, varying the philosophy of what makes the optimal quota. I can say with confidence that fewer get this more "right" than others. No one tries to make it perfect; as long as it feels right to leadership and they can explain it with confidence, they can pitch it to their sellers. The seller then accepts, per the role requirement, and "makes it rain."

Quotas suffer from both poor logic in their financial calculation as well as human elements that negatively impact success. Poor logic could be anything from just dividing the overall budget by the number of sellers, selecting quota values without understanding historical data or forecasted pipeline, or poorly vetting factors or weightings, to name the most common problems.

Human elements are a bit different than the other elements and can be tricky. Let me explain a few of the human elements at play and provide a quick way to avoid the risk:

- **Individuals responsible for calculating compensation plan and quota have never actually been in a selling role or worked directly with customers.** They do not know the little things that could impact or influence outcomes.

» **Fix:** Assemble a team of individuals that includes the head of sales, at least two regional leaders of sales, and a portion of your most respected sellers to create the logics. Including experts and respected peers of the quota recipients will provide validation that the quota concepts were sound.

- **Overthinking the calculations and metrics.** Simplicity with quotas is best for sellers, while complex is best for the company.

    » **Fix:** Regardless of your company's size and number of offerings, sellers sell more when they clearly understand their plan. Keep it simple: sellers sell XX in dollars and companies pay XX% against that. Once the company adds such elements as matrices, calculations per offering, and thresholds to be met, it becomes clear that the seller is intended to sell more yet earn less. Keep the cocktail-napkin rule in mind. The quota is intended to increase sales performance, not show how smart MBAs are at making it complex.

- **Not correctly accounting for elements such as sales cycles, win rates, historical purchasing patterns, past sales performance, market changes, resource availability, delivery and service capabilities, or timing of business changes.**

    » **Fix:** Always understand the individual historical metrics related to customer, seller, products, capabilities and market. The trends this can show will easily allow for the right people to get the right quotas for greatest outcomes

- **Focusing the quota allocation on specific product offerings yet the business desiring achievement in differing growth areas of capabilities.** An example would be a company who sells a lot of equipment, with a quota based on those sales, that wants dramatic increases in service-based offerings with a minimal quota element tied to that portion of the business.

    » **Fix:** All too often a compensation plan heavily leans toward a single core offering. But some in the company make a living selling non-core offerings and cannot be successful unless those selling the core offerings properly sell within the broader portfolio. Companies make tweaks to allow for non-core, but tweaks demonstrate that you are not serious about desiring results. If you plan to have multiple elements or weightings in a plan, make them balanced—don't make them 90% core and 10% non-core if you really want more non-core sold. Sellers sell based on what their quota will pay them most for. Balanced is best for greatest outcomes.

- **Friendships or favorites leaders deem as "best" sellers with more favorable quota allocations.** This occurs across nearly all organizations and businesses to some degree.

    » **Fix:** I provide a longer discussion below, but nepotism, friends, and "favorite" sellers can blind leaders at quota time. Blindness and disproportional quotas lead to lesser attainment for the leader at year's end.

- **Improper communication and messaging of the plan construct and intended benefits.**

    » **Fix:** At regular intervals during the creation process, hold reviews with a broader sales audience to gain their feedback. This allows you to learn nuances that might have been overlooked prior to finalizing your plans. Once the plans are released, hold a well-structured review with all sales, making sure there is a definitive rationale for how each intended plan element and benefit will resonate.

It is also best to reaffirm the use of historical data points and the expert team you created to help craft the plans.

I've seen all of the problems in the list above in action. Regardless of other issues at a company, I have little doubt that there is always some human element playing a role when quotas do not fit the company strategy.

Some Traditional Human Elements to Overcome

Did you ever wonder how some of the same people end up winning top performer awards at the company kickoff every year? We are told it is due to their consistency in achieving at the highest levels, which is what makes them the best sellers. But how is that possible if they support the same customers and receive an annual growth number in their annual quota allocation while you struggle to reach the top? There is likely more behind the curtain than leadership has divulged, but what leadership seems to not give the seller credit for is eyesight and common sense. Sellers are not blind. When favors clearly place one seller in the limelight and the other in the doghouse, or when one seller earns more money, recognition, or rewards while others struggle to find an equal opportunity for the same level of success based on skill and effort rather than favor, it creates major distrust and demotivates the team.

If a seller is consistently on stage, let's have a look to see if their quota grows annually in proportion to what is expected of them or others. If that individual can attain their quota just by selling the same base business they sell annually and not be required to sell $xxx in net new growth sales when the rest of the team is, that is a problem, farmer managing a relationship or not. Even someone who is managing a long-term customer relationship should have to achieve some measurement of success to expand the customer growth, whether in dollars or by meeting some other objective. That seller who is simply retaining the customer relationship at the same base revenue year over year should not "earn" them an award at the annual kickoff by just sustaining and not growing the business in some meaningful way compared to others growth objectives. I've seen this type of seller called onto the stage at countless companies, yet when I ask why, I have been told that their customer is very important to the company, and the customer really likes their seller, so they cannot afford to lose the seller. While placing that seller on stage might motivate them, however, it is at the risk of making other sellers feel less valued.

How much is existing pipeline being considered during the quota creation process? I had an experience with a company that had a seller finalize a service sale in month two of the new fiscal year. That sale immediately placed the seller at 105% of their entire annual quota; their year was attained in one deal that was in their sales pipeline when the quotas were being defined. This example shows that the existing pipeline was either not considered in the quota creation at all or leadership was determined to allow the individual to overachieve for the year. The only other option would be that the seller intentionally hid the deal in the pipeline or downplayed the reality of the opportunity to keep quota creators from using it in the calculation—but for a deal at the assigned quota level size to close so quickly in the new year, the sales leader would have had to know the deal was nearing closure.

Obviously this is a great situation for the seller, who is now at 105% of quota with ten months remaining in the year. That seller's motivation however is now set to autopilot; they close out the fiscal year 10 months later at 150% of attainment and are guaranteed a spot on stage and a membership in the president's club. The same seller might have been able to achieve 30-50% higher revenue for their company had they been provided a more properly allocated quota against their true pipeline and business potential.

You may ask, "So what? Who gets hurt?" The casualty here is a culture based on fairness. If anyone on a sales team, in this case the seller attaining 150%, is allocated a relatively soft number compared to their customer base and pipeline potential when they could have carried a more aligned quota, other team members are responsible for taking on higher quotas to make up the difference. Of course, this all implies that many sellers do not drive sales as hard after they have achieved 100% of their annual quota obligation as they had during the pursuit of 100%. I hold firm to that inference. I have seen many sellers back their foot off the gas pedal once they reach the comfort zone of being safe in their quota attainment for the year. Some may still push hard if their quota supports overachievement payouts and a financial benefit exists, but others will hold deals until the next fiscal year when they know they will need them more. Less often do I see sellers push as hard as they had prior to 100%. So showing any level of favor towards a seller who has a base of customers with greater potential limits the company's opportunity for higher sales growth and hurts the rest of the team.

Consider also that allocating a larger quota to a seller with a smaller base of customers or less favorable geographic potential for increased sales growth has the adverse effect for the company. If that individual carries more quota than their potential can bear, the seller will be at risk of losing motivation—or worse, leaving the company altogether prior to year-end. Both have negative consequences for the company:

- **Lost motivation equates to lesser sales than they could have achieved with a more aligned quota.** The seller now incurs lower attainment to quota, which leads to less earning opportunity if quota is based on a % of attainment, a lower chance to achieve president's club, and very likely a low-performing spot on the company wide stack rankings. This is unfair when we consider that in fact they might not have been a low performer had the quotas been properly allocated based on market potential. This is not new and occurs within nearly every company across every industry. What is the result? The 45% who fall short of their quota fail in the eyes of executives, feel less motivated, and are less desirous to work for an environment that does not provide an equal opportunity for success.
- If the seller leaves the company, it creates a void in sales capacity, and the company is no longer driving new sales at all against an uncovered quota. This leads to the likelihood of $0.00 in sales closed for that open role as well as a list of unhappy customers that could be at risk if they feel neglected while you find a new seller. Could another team member assist while you find a replacement? Yes, but then they are likely neglecting other opportunities or no longer building a more robust pipeline for themselves. It is an ugly cycle that can be prevented with a balanced plan allocation.

Consider the costs associated with lost potential. If the company now pays a favored employee at a higher rate beyond 100% attainment due to overachievement of quota, the company might pay an extra 1-2 percentage points for that overachievement value when it was not properly earned. Some might argue that other sellers fell short of quota, so the company makes it back by paying less to them; perhaps you did pay less in commission to those individuals, but at what cost to the business? Were more skilled resources incorrectly applied to the opportunities the favored employee supported as opposed to assisting on other important opportunities that have now been lost? How much revenue and profit were lost for the company in those opportunities? Do underachieving sellers, who might be the right people in the wrong circumstance, now desire to leave, thus creating a need to recruit new employees to backfill? What about the employees who supported the other lost deals and also lost the possibility of earning some level of commission or bonus based on supporting engagements?

This also extends beyond the sales team. At most companies the effort of selling can have a ripple effect across every single employee in the company, including those in finance, HR, procurement, recruitment, technical support, and more. All employees have something at risk if sellers are not best able to sell to their true potential. The costs of recruitment, the onboarding of employees, and the time required to establish relationships and grow a pipeline are high for a business. Yet all that could have been avoided by simply establishing a fair and balanced quota process that favored the customers and company.

So who gets hurt? Everyone except the individual seller who received the favor stands to get hurt. And per Aristotle, "The whole is more than the sum of its parts." Do not make one person happy at the risk of the many. The costs are far too great than what you stand to receive.

Beyond Traditional Thinking

What if no quota were assigned? What if the quota was truly $0.00? Does selling stop? Is a quota really what motivate sellers to sell at the highest levels of achievement, or is having the right leaders with the right people all you need? I am confident most sellers generate more sales when high levels of customer satisfaction and employee satisfaction exist than from an allocated quota of any value.

Be thoughtful about your response to this. Executives might say, "Of course selling would stop or fall significantly!" I am willing to bet, however, that there would be a large base of sellers and sales leaders who disagree. I am one. So, who is right—the executive who might not understand sales in general or a sellers motivating factors and thinks everyone must have a number dangling over their head to be successful, or the sales leaders and sellers who hate the misdirected pressure a quota places on them and trust that without a quota they will be more successful? How often does a company not allocate new quotas to sellers until Q2 of the new fiscal year? Do sales completely stop until the quotas are in a seller's hand? The answer is no. Sellers continue to sell and support customers. Yet, some companies will pause paying commission to sellers until the new quotas are complete. Ironic right? Sellers still sell with or without a quota in hand yet companies won't pay without a quota defined. A quota the seller does not play a role in creating. So again, who exactly needs a quota in place to be willing to do their job?

My years of experience leaves me confident having a quota is perfectly fine—it's not necessary to eliminate it altogether—but if you apply a quota based on the right strategy and measured properly against rationale sales expectations, your results will equal **more revenue, more profit, more attainment against the company budget, and more success at attaining and retaining top talent with a higher determination to achieve success**. This all stems from creating a smart strategy, as discussed in Chapter 10, the *less is more* idea that has been the very basis for my ideas, methods, and principles for success.

Let me share an experience with a business I was assisting years ago, but it is important to note this example is not unlike the patterns many companies experience as traditional quota setting methods. When I began working with the company I quickly assessed that they did not have a sales and personnel problem so much as a strategy and supporting-quota problem. (It's important to note here that once a new strategy was defined, the sales model and personnel supporting it could certainly have become a business issue, but blaming them at the moment was unreasonable, as so many other elements of the business were misaligned for success.) The business was selling advanced technologies. Their product and brand were well known in the industry, yet the industry was evolving and equipment alone was less profitable and in less demand. Like so many other companies, the organization was faced with transforming into a provider of services and solutions, as opposed to equipment alone, or the business growth would erode until they were unable to operate and exist financially. A decision was made by executives to undertake the change, yet they were predominantly structured to sell product, and the existing employees lacked the deeper knowledge to run a business designed around properly implementing services or solutions. After several years of unsuccessfully trying to transform their business, my responsibility was to evaluate their efforts and help them progress toward the future.

Now, many structural elements related to their business model and the rights defined within this book needed to evolve (my polite way of saying "needed to be ripped out and replaced"), but for this example I will speak just to what I believe from a quota perspective diminished their ability to change the current annual trend of revenue losses they were experiencing. The total business revenue had decreased at a rate of approximately 10-20% per year from what should have been a comfortable positive growth in sales in a marketplace in which their brand had been well respected.

The existing quota method they were using to change from a product led company to a service and solution provider was the following. The existing product sellers would begin to sell services (managed services, professional services, break/fix, and maintenance) in addition to product. Each person carried the same $5M quota per person they held for product, with the same up-to-6% commission per revenue dollar sold. Yup, that's it. Zero changes to the quota methodology other than to add that there was a need to sell services in their discussions with customers. No defined strategy or business planning, no training, no significant change in personnel, nothing other than the message "We now sell services. Go sell!" I am sure the executives believed there was more to it than what I just stated, but quota and commission percentages were what was driving the selling team, nothing more. This sounds unbelievable to conceive, yet is not uncommon as a business considers the need to evolve their business but applies little understanding or financial investment on how to achieve best outcomes.

Allow me to share my immediate assessment as it related to quota, pipeline and sales motivation. I could tell I wasn't their favorite person right away. First I asked the following two questions:

1. "How many sales—product, service, or both—does it take for a seller to attain $5M in sales based on your average sale price?"
2. "Can I have access to your pipeline reports, including past two years' win-loss reports?"

The first hurdle in my assessment is always to leverage historical data to evaluate existing from past sales and/or purchasing history. Many companies today utilize SalesForce as their CRM for pipeline-

and bookings-based reporting along with a wealth of financial-based reports. This company was set up similarly, but as is the case with so many, their use of SalesForce varied between users, thus making data analysis more challenging. In those last 12 months, they had a service win rate of just 25% and a loss rate of 75%. (Note: For my assessment, I do include opportunities abandoned or undecided as part of the loss rate, as those opportunities were initially pursued yet now no longer exist.)

Additionally, specific only to the services they sold, their average value for a win was $39,000 and their average value for a loss was $164,000. So, the value of their losses was four times that of their win value. They also won a very low percentage of the time—for me, it takes something nearer to a 50% win rate for most companies to be successful at achieving their financial goals. One very positive data point to consider here is that they had $164,000 in the "average" loss, which means larger opportunities did in fact exist with the potential to be won. That is important as it demonstrates the right potential for success exists.

For product, the win-loss percentage did not change, but what is important to know is that the sales price of their single most expensive product offering was approximately $500,000 to $750,000. One last metric I will add is that the sales cycle for the average product sale was approximately 6-12 months, but when it was sold as a solution (product + service), the sales cycle could increase to 1-3 months depending on the added complexity. Detrimental for both a seller's quota attainment and a company's achievement of expanding into new offerings.

It was not hard to see numerous issues at play with respect to quota, motivating factors, and existing sales outcomes. Not only were the sellers not motivated to add services to their equipment sales, as it only added more time to the sales process, but the service added no financial benefit to their ability to reach their annual quota. After all, the service value was only $39,000 per deal based on those deals they won. Forget for a moment that they were losing services opportunities that averaged $164,000, which is sizable; yet in their minds, this only proved that they could not win deals at that value. From their perspective, selling services was too small a value to add 1-3 months per sales cycle to their product sales. Mathematically, the sellers also knew that based on their existing customer base, prospective customers, the number of deals they could reasonably close within a year, and the sales cycle, the potential for reaching $5M at all was nearly impossible. As is often the case with most sellers with a large quota, they quickly determined that selling the highest-valued product for $750,000 in the most-timely manner was in their best interest if they wanted to reach 100% of their quota attainment. The result was that the sellers sold product primarily and most still missed their quotas. So sellers missed their quotas, lost commissions, and became dejected while the company also continued to lose money year over year and did not grow sales for services, all because the quota did not mathematically, nor logically, align with the product values or sales cycles for selling a broader portfolio of offerings. They simply misunderstood the power of the right quota for achieving the desired outcomes. Let's not forget what is most important. The customer was not provided the full breadth of available options their vendor had for supporting their business needs. Customer relationships weaken over time with this method of engagement.

Do I blame the sellers for selling just the highest-priced product? No. They were never trained or properly equipped to sell a service or solution, so they lacked the skills necessary to embrace what would lead to success. They were also provided a quota that would have been difficult to attain even if they sold at a win rate of 50%, which most were not doing. Add to this that the company lacked the right culture and right mindset across the business to be successful in the evolution to services. Very similar to how many companies operate in similar transformations.

I also do not place much blame on sales leadership here, as they were told to find a way to get to budget attainment without any changes in strategy, business plans, sales go-to-market, expertise, personnel, customers, or mindset. They were destined to fall short on day one of the next fiscal year. And worst of all for the sellers, they knew it.

Allow me to share another example of why quota matters and how important it is for sales leadership to play a more significant role. Years ago, I was asked to lead a strategic services business that included both cloud-based services and managed/outsourcing services. The two types of services were quite different in terms of sales methodology, trained selling skills, prospective customers, and sales pricing. Pricing for cloud services ranged in value from $500 per month to as much as $20,000 or more per month, while IT outsourcing services for that company ranged from $500,000 annually to $10M annually.

Here were the initial flaws I faced with this model:
- I was informed after creating the business model that instead of having enough of a personnel budget to hire two distinct selling teams, we would have to hire a single team that was responsible for selling all the offerings as a combined portfolio of services.
- My overall team budget as a sales leader was allocated at an amount that more greatly favored the need to sell outsourcing-based services at a much higher sale value. It was

addressed, and the response was to just go sell and make the budget. What I heard, of course, was "make the budget."

None of this pleased me as a sales leader, but it was time to turn lemons into lemonade. Even though I had not felt I was given the proper headcount, I still decided to allocate quotas amongst the team based on some sellers being cloud specialists and the rest outsourcing specialists. This enabled me to better allocate fair quota values based on their specialty while also incenting each seller to cross-sell in the other specialty. This avoided making selling both too onerous but still covered the extra quota. I shared my rationale with the sellers, and all were comfortable with the way the quotas were distributed. This meant they either trusted me or the quota values appeared reasonable enough to make quota, so I knew my balance must have been fair.

The new year began and we quickly identified our first quandary. The public cloud service was relatively new to the marketplace, so the customer community had yet to accept and adopt to this new technology over their existing way of doing business. In other words, my sellers were doing a lot of customer education on what cloud was capable of doing, but were not closing deals as most customers still did not want to risk their careers on a relatively unproven technology. Public cloud sales began to struggle and fall behind on expectations. The sellers immediately focused more attention on the managed/outsourcing offerings, as the budget and their quotas still allowed for cross-selling of our offerings. The good news is that managed/outsourcing was then selling at the proper rate, but public cloud was at a slow crawl (to be frank, it stopped).

I received a call from the executive I reported to, who quickly told me that the global COO was not pleased with public cloud sales performance. I explained that while I agreed it needed to improve, the market was facing a learning curve. We were addressing this curve while also finding ways to make a living for all involved, including ensuring overall company financial success. This was not the response he wanted to hear, and he told me immediately to have one seller begin spending his time cold calling for public cloud in the mornings and selling outsourcing in the afternoons.

I explained that approach would have no positive end result for the seller, me as a leader, nor he as an executive, as we would all fail. I continued to explain that the seller has an individual quota of $10M and public cloud sold for $500 per month per virtual machine. The average public cloud sale is only $1,200 per month or $14,400 annually. If we focused on this, it would be mathematically impossible for any of us to make our assigned quotas. I would rather miss sales expectations on one service element than miss them all due to my focusing my best people on selling less-than-optimal solutions. He disagreed, I did not, and the call ended. I stuck with my plan.

Was I being a difficult employee by not following the direction of my executive? Possibly. But in my opinion, I was much closer to the problem than he, and I could not risk the success of the entire business due to a fearful gut reaction from a conversation with a global COO who was located in another country and not close enough to the market challenge. I also was highly confident that the quota allocation modifications I had made to the original business plan were right, and I trusted my ability to make it a success for all involved.

Fast forward to the end of the year. This new group did underperform in their attainment of the total sales revenue expected for public cloud units sold. It was a miss, and I owned that. We did, however, add public cloud to every sale we made for managed services and outsourcing, so all was not lost, and we now had customer references and live use cases for public cloud while also proving a market did exist.

However, the budget was created based on the consolidated services from all the strategic services we offered, not by individual offering alone. My team had achieved 148% of the budget, and I along with one of my team members made president's club that year. I was also awarded the designation of Top at Large Leader.

I'm not using the awards as rationale for why others should challenge a direct order from an executive. I would never recommend someone risk their reputation or their career potential as I did. I do, however, believe that leaders are hired to be leaders. It is a leader's responsibility to own and control the desired outcomes the company defined for that year. I was confident in my strategy and unwilling to place the success of the entire business at risk. As a leader, I remained committed to the plan I had defined. While public cloud had fallen short of expectations, it had created improved awareness among the executive team that simply throwing a revenue number out based on what you want the success to be for that service, rather than considering all the influencers that new products face, can be catastrophic to the success of a business. Had the strategy been developed first, prior to that number being defined in the budget, they likely would have uncovered the risks, and better choices might have been made. Regardless, the company made their desired financial achievement, which stood out to me as more important than selling any one offering over another.

What do my years of experience tell me about the best methodology for quota setting? In short, that we should stop setting random or unrealistic quotas and better enforce the right leaders to lead. I do not personally trust that quotas motivate or drive outcomes as others do. Much of this has to do with many organizations not taking the quota creation process as seriously as they should and applying better rigor and fairness across the entire company, as explained throughout this chapter. I have witnessed myself, and heard others speak about, far too many situations in which quota numbers were picked seemingly at random.

I also feel that many leaders do not fully consider what does motivate and how changes in the psychology of quota allocation can more greatly drive higher results. Consider how many of the truly skilled top sellers in companies, those who consistently exceed their quota attainment, would tell you that they do not pay much attention to their quota beyond the day it is assigned and the last day of the fiscal year. Numerous sellers (including myself) have stated that thinking about the number gets in the way of their success. This is primarily due to the best sellers and sales leaders knowing they will be successful because they will sell and win as much as they can regardless of a number assigned to them. The number for many is a minimum, not a maximum.

A Better Concept for Quota Allocation

That said, here is a philosophy on quota setting for maximum outcomes. Let's use the $5M quota mentioned earlier as the example. As you recall, that quota was a number the company needed from every seller to reach unrealistic growth with a poorly defined strategy in an evolving business. In essence, it was the initial budget number divided by the number of sellers. Yet the $5M had an adverse effect on the transformation from a product-focused sales team to that of a service-and-solutions sales team. This $5M was well beyond the standard "stretch number" for most sellers. The result was that sellers only focused on the highest-priced product, and most sellers missed their targets quite significantly, as did the sales leader and the entire business.

A better model for this example would have been no quota at all. That's right—$0.00 of assigned quota per seller, and I firmly believe the company would have recognized a significant increase in revenue above what the $5M per seller had generated. In addition to the $0.00, apply the proper level of sales leadership to provide oversight to the right strategic plans, the right people, the right customers along with the right solutions, and success will follow. If a quota does not incent, add benefit, or if it detracts from creating revenue growth, then do not have it.

Now, I appreciate that no executive with a multi-million-dollar budget is going to jump on board with a $0.00 quota per seller. That's what I will refer to as an institutionalized mentality (or should I refer back to the definition of insanity?). I can hear executives now saying something like, "Quotas are used in every company worldwide, have been assigned for decades, and are at the core of how companies measure seller success and motivate. I have never heard of not assigning a seller a quota. Are you kidding?"

I am not. I am stating that we use them because that is how it has always been done, plain and simple. That old logic alone does not demonstrate the company's desire to achieve more. The world is changing in so many ways, and leaders in a business have to evolve their thinking alongside that. We should be evolving our strategies, how we calculate quotas—and yes, challenging the idea that a number even matters more than the strategy itself.

Tables 8 and 9 on the following page are a comparison of the results we get when we allocate $5M in quota to a seller versus a lesser quota value. Since the $0.00 quota is a difficult concept for many to feel confident about, apply a quota of just $2M-3M to every seller. Frankly, I believe $1M is all you need. This allows for a measurable outcome and provides HR a rational measurement for performance management purposes. More importantly, you will generate more revenue across the broader portfolio of offerings as well as profit.

Consider the two tables I provided as examples for supporting the lower quota concept. Below are my analyses of several key areas.

- **Table 8: Existing Quota Model**

    This table is based on the $5M quota allocation.
    - » Overall attainment to quota across the team is 51% for the sales leader, a significant shortfall.
    - » Only 1 of the 10 sellers have achieved over their $5M quota. This will lead to dissatisfied employees who may consider employment elsewhere. If they stay, they will be less motivated to succeed.
    - » Little, if any, achievement of the new service and solution initiative has been attained due to the focus on higher-valued product with long sales cycles.
    - » In many business environments, sales toward the end of the year begin to slow down as those sellers who know they cannot meet quota will hold deals to begin the next fiscal year off strong.
    - » Sellers will focus on what matters to them most in order to achieve quota, as opposed to the needs of the customer, as a relationship sale is designed to do. In this case, they chose to focus on the $750,000 product as opposed to the smaller and longer sales cycle service. This creates a loss in revenue, customer intimacy, and satisfaction.

- **Table 9: New Quota Model**

    This table is based on a quota allocation of just $2M-3M per seller.
    - » Overall attainment to quota is 121% for the sales leader.

TABLE 8: EXISTING QUOTA MODEL ($5M PER SELLER)

	JAN	FEB	MAR	APRIL	MAY	JUNE	JULY	AUG	SEPT	OCT
Seller 1	750,000	-	-	-	750,000	1,310,000	-	775,000	-	675,000
Seller 2	-	-	730,000	-		720,000	1,230,000	-	-	1,290,000
Seller 3	-	520,000	560,000	-	-	550,000	-	650,000	-	-
Seller 4	650,000	-	-	510,000	-	475,000	-	-	-	590,000
Seller 5	520,000	-	-	710,000	-	-	1,320,000	-	-	-
Seller 6	-	-	575,000	-	-	410,000	-	600,000	750,000	-
Seller 7	-	-	350,000	510,000	-	475,000	-	-	400,000	-
Seller 8	-	330,000	-	-	-	-	650,000	575,000	-	-
Seller 9	-	-	650,000	-	-	375,000	-	100,000	-	60,000
Seller 10	-	210,000	-	-	250,000	-	-	200,000	-	160,000
Totals	1,920,000	1,060,000	2,865,000	1,730,000	1,000,000	4,315,000	3,200,000	2,900,000	1,150,000	2,775,000

TABLE 9: NEW QUOTA MODEL ($2M-$3M PER SELLER)

	JAN	FEB	MAR	APRIL	MAY	JUNE	JULY	AUG	SEPT	OCT
Seller 1	750,000	-	-	-	750,000	1,310,000	-	775,000	-	675,000
Seller 2	-	-	730,000	-		720,000	1,230,000	-	-	1,290,000
Seller 3	-	520,000	560,000	40,000	210,000	280,000	60,000	370,000	-	1,290,000
Seller 4	650,000	60,000	70,000	510,000	250,000	475,000	130,000	48,000	575,000	95,000
Seller 5	520,000	60,000	140,000	710,000	360,000	175,000	30,000	210,000	310,000	-
Seller 6	72,000	50,000	575,000	75,000	45,000	450,000	-	700,000	380,000	50,000
Seller 7	-	110,000	350,000	510,000	375,000	190,000	60,000	100,000	90,000	-
Seller 8	80,000	180,000	40,000	10,000	175,000	30,000	650,000	575,000	-	100,000
Seller 9	30,000	210,000	650,000	60,000	45,000	375,000	-	230,000	30,000	60,000
Seller 10	30,000	210,000	150,000	60,000	250,000	135,000	120,000	220,000	30,000	160,000
Totals	2,132,000	1,400,000	3,265,000	1,975,000	2,460,000	4,140,000	2,280,000	3,228,000	1,415,000	3,720,000

*Note: Charts are examples of results that can be achieved by applying a different logic to quota setting

NOV	DEC	TOTALS	QUOTA	PERCENT OF QUOTA	AVG DEAL VALUE	AVG REV PER MONTH	BLENDED MARGIN %
-	889,000	5,149,000	5,000,000	103%	858,167	429,083	15%
580,000	-	4,550,000	5,000,000	91%	910,000	379,167	14%
650,000	-	2,930,000	5,000,000	59%	586,000	244,167	10%
-	475,000	2,700,000	5,000,000	54%	540,000	225,000	12%
-	-	2,550,000	5,000,000	51%	850,000	212,500	12%
-	-	2,335,000	5,000,000	47%	583,750	194,583	13%
-	-	1,735,000	5,000,000	35%	433,750	144,583	17%
-	-	1,555,000	5,000,000	31%	518,333	129,583	18%
-	-	1,185,000	5,000,000	24%	296,250	98,750	10%
-	-	820,000	5,000,000	16%	205,000	68,333	16%
1,230,000	1,364,000	25,509,000	50,000,000	51%	578,125	2,125,750	14%

NOV	DEC	TOTALS	QUOTA	PERCENT OF QUOTA	AVG DEAL VALUE	AVG REV PER MONTH	BLENDED MARGIN %	REVENUE GROWTH
-	889,000	5,149,000	3,000,000	172%	858,167	429,083	15%	0%
580,000	-	4,550,000	3,000,000	152%	910,000	379,167	14%	0%
275,000	155,000	3,760,000	3,000,000	125%	376,000	313,333	16%	22%
250,000	75,000	3,188,000	3,000,000	106%	265,667	265,667	18%	15%
250,000	75,000	2,840,000	2,000,000	142%	258,182	236,667	18%	10%
70,000	80,000	2,547,000	2,000,000	127%	231,545	212,250	19%	8%
110,000	10,000	1,905,000	2,000,000	95%	190,500	158,750	25%	9%
30,000	-	1,870,000	2,000,000	94%	187,000	155,833	24%	17%
-	75,000	1,765,000	2,000,000	88%	176,500	147,083	21%	33%
50,000	75,000	1,490,000	2,000,000	75%	124,167	124,167	25%	45%
1,615,000	1,434,000	29,064,000	24,000,000	121%	357,773	2,422,000	20%	12%

- 6 out of 10 sellers, or 60%, achieved sales above their quota.
- Overall sales revenue increased by 12% for the business compared to that of the $5M quota allocation results.
- Average revenue being generated per month also increased by 12% for the business overall.
- Average deal value decreased but as a result of less is more, sales and margins rose, as did customer satisfaction.
- The addition of services not only increased revenue but also positively grew profit from a higher margin service offering to compliment the lower margin product sales. Average margin per sale increased by 6% as more services were sold with higher margins per offering.
- Note also that this model shows an increase in sales revenue 9 out of the 12 months compared to that of the $5M quota allocation results. The benefits of more monthly services being sold, along with increasing the values of deals sold within the existing table, as individuals are more willing to attach more offerings even if sales cycles slow slightly. This improves not only the expanded breadth of offerings, but also increases monthly revenue flow that can be used for other investments. In most cases, monthly revenue that is based on annuitized service that will be guaranteed year after year.
- While individual sellers increase their earnings, the company increased commissions per seller aligned with increased revenue growth for the company. Overachievement formulas did not negatively impact the company

but actually earned them more overall due to increased revenue sold at higher margin values.
» Overall, sales revenue grew, company profit grew, sellers increased their success rate and customer relationships strengthened.

The table comparisons are samples, but are based on a business I assisted that was experiencing similar outcomes to those shown within Table 8. The unreasonableness of the original budget creation that leads to the trickle-down effect for seller quotas can be so erroneous in concept that it is as though the company drives their own hearse to the cemetery and just waits for fate to arrive. True sellers get into sales because they are competitive and want to earn money by selling. They are naturally self-motivated, as discussed earlier within this chapter. Capture that motivation by understanding what drives them and do not create boundaries to limit their potential. The $5M quota per seller in this example was so ambitious that it was highly detrimental to seller motivation and the ability to understand the customer and benefit

> *True sellers are naturally self-motivated... capture that motivation by understanding what drives them and do not create boundaries to limit their potential.*

from a true customer relationship, and of course created an outcome where most involved failed and would experience the effects of that failure well into the future. Companies cannot recover from such mistakes overnight, and in a case like this, sales will suffer for some time.

I am not conceptually stating do not give quotas. I am stating that companies need to stop believing bigger quotas must be better and will produce increased outcomes. I am also not ignoring that my approach does not take into account the overall company budget when allocating the $2M-3M per seller. I simply believe that the quotas do not have to mathematically calculate to companywide value or else the company will not be successful. I believe it will achieve greater results for many companies if they do not. Smarter quotas with the right leadership and right people will expand your potential for success far more.

Most companies are not built on a team of what some consider A-level sellers with the most experience and best selling skills. Maybe a few exist on the team, but most teams have a combination of A, B and C sellers. If you do not train them, provide them the proper leadership and skilled resources to be successful, or align them for success with all the rights discussed in this book, they will underperform. And their failure should be an inquiry of leadership, who has overlooked the ability to achieve greatness because of a mathematical calculation not the sole fault of an individual seller.

You need to consider some important and relevant questions:

Does the quota, as defined and formulated, drive momentum for best outcomes?

Will the quota increase the desired behavior? This is especially important to understand in a transformational environment.

Can the quota increase wrong behavior as defined? If so, what wrong behaviors might occur?

What is my selling strategy? Was it a strategy to meet the quota or a quota to meet the strategy?

One closing thought: Consider what occurs with right quotas versus incorrectly defined quotas, especially when provided to less-than-qualified sellers and sales leaders. Does the weight of a quota make the seller, experienced or inexperienced, an unappealing representative of your company for the customer to build a relationship with? Faced with a difficult quota, sellers can become intolerable and pushy, focusing only on POs based on what matters to their earnings versus the true customer needs. Customers can feel that pressure and—likely in more cases than we want to admit—buy less. As sellers and sales leaders, we all know that we have lost customers in the past. What needs to be assured is that we do not lose opportunities due to unnatural pressures applied by the same people who incorrectly defined our quota.

Applying the Rights with Attainment of Budget (Specific to Sales Leaders)

This section was written to assist sales leaders in their ability to overachieve their budget. I will speak specifically about properly applying what you have learned throughout this book about the rights, making the leadership choices that will lead to your most optimal approach, and budget allocation across your right people. Your choices can be the differentiator in your ability to either overachieve your budget or fall well below. The good news is that the choices and the power to make those choices are firmly in your hands. The bad news is that as a leader, you must come forward and make strong confident decisions based solely on the success of your team, your business, and of course, you.

Dissecting your budget number should be relatively simple, but the fact is these decisions can often cause leaders to lose sleep, friends at work, or even their jobs. This is exactly why I want to assist you in making smart decisions. You have already gained valuable knowledge by reading the rights within this book, and it is my hope that your confidence in making the best decisions for your success should feel much clearer.

I am about to share two separate graphs. The purpose of each will be to show you how a budget attainment applied with the right choices would look in comparison to a budget attainment that maintains the status quo and involves no modifications to align it with the rights.

Table 10 describes decisions that need to be made upon receiving your new team budget. The table is designed to demonstrate the change in allocation percentage that occurs as you make each decision, which either improves your ability to attain 100% or more of your assigned team budget achievement or may negatively impact your ability to attain 100%. The columns provided for both revenue and profit enable you to see the small risk or benefit that occurs when each decision is enacted. As you can see, in the first table decisions are made wisely, and each improves your opportunity to ensure your overall success before ever allocating quotas to your team members. The line graph shown in Chart 2 is provided so that you can visualize the positive effects your decisions can make on your quota attainment for the year. Let's review and compare each.

TABLE 10: RIGHT CHOICES

ATTAINMENT TO PLAN CHART (RIGHT CHOICES)		
100% REVENUE	100% PROFIT	DECISION
100%	100%	Hired two new employees 3 months prior to new FY
103%	101%	Gained higher skill sellers but maintained budget payroll
105%	102%	Reallocated account base to more aligned skills
106%	103%	Pipeline and sales cycle affords 12 months of selling due to timing
106%	104%	Sellers offer broader portfolio of offerings with higher value
106%	103%	Clients request cost reduction but due to higher value has slightly less impact to profit
107%	103%	Skills training occurs
107%	98%	Market shifts and equipments costs increase

CHART 2: RIGHT CHOICES

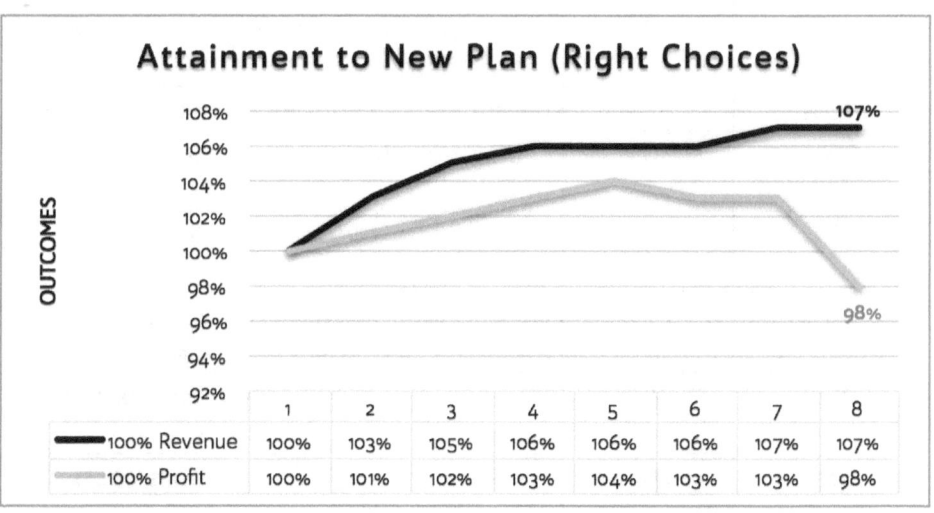

Table 11 represents what a business can look like prior to quota allocation if the sales leader makes decisions not aligned to the rights within the book but simply retains more of a status-quo approach with human elements we discussed earlier to the allocation process. I appreciate that some reading this book may want to question my method and the rationale behind the percentage of change. Understand that I am not stating that my sample percentages within Table 11 are perfectly aligned to your specific company budget or team model. All teams' budgets, headcounts, and the variation based on those will differ based on the individual company. What I am asking is that you be honest with yourself and consider the relevance of the message. Consider the impact it might have on your sellers' ability to meet their quota, your ability to meet your budget, and the company's ability to achieve corporate-wide expectations.

TABLE 11: STATUS QUO

ATTAINMENT TO NEW PLAN (STATUS QUO)		
100% REVENUE	100% PROFIT	DECISION
98%	98%	Hired lesser skilled person for selling role
98%	97%	Lesser person has higher than average salary, higher cost
98%	95%	Lesser person requires assistance
96%	90%	Did same related to two team members
90%	80%	Hire late for two open roles. Pipeline growth slow
88%	77%	No changes to client base. Want cost reduction yet costs increase
85%	74%	No training or tools enhancement to save costs
85%	70%	Market shifts and equipments costs increase

CHART 3: STATUS QUO

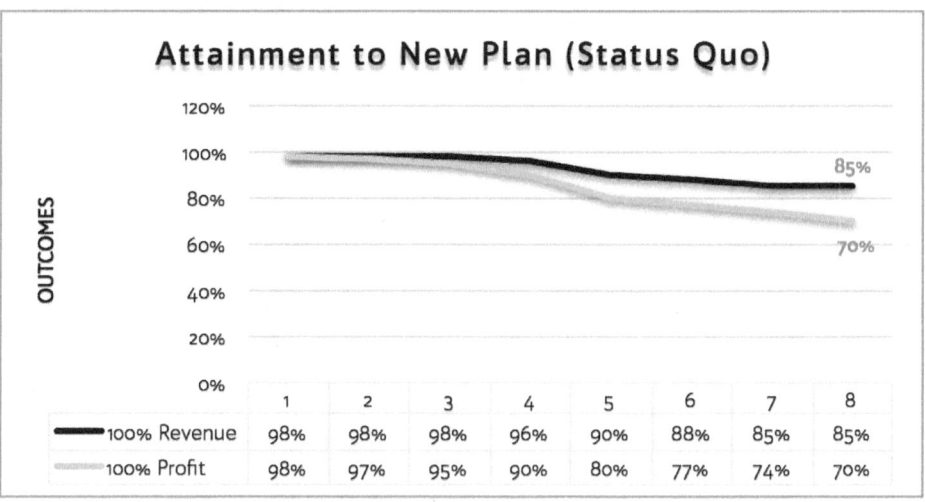

When you as a sales leader have the opportunity to make more educated choices that can most greatly impact the success (or failure) of your business, why wouldn't you consider what is being depicted? Especially when you know how many unknowns may pop up throughout the year that you simply cannot control? If you have the benefit of making smarter leadership choices before the fiscal year begins, you should personally see that as your first opportunity to solidify success for your business. These valuable choices, far more than quota, determine your potential for success.

Results are more greatly impacted by employee satisfaction, customer satisfaction and the choices described within this book, not a quota being allocated. As leaders, you have the power to make those choices along with creating the resulting outcomes.

Chapter 15

BUILD A CULTURE THAT'S RIGHT FOR YOU

Best Outcomes Come from Best Attitudes

MAYA ANGELOU IS KNOWN for an incredibly meaningful quote that applies across all society but especially stands out to me in a sales capacity. It reads, "People will forget what you said, people will forget what you did, but people will never forget how you made them feel."

As sellers and sales leaders, you have to recognize the value the right culture brings to your potential for success. I recall the global CEO, of Dimension Data, Brett Dawson, regularly stating, "You build competitive businesses through winning cultures." This applies to your team, the personnel across your entire company, and of course your customers and partners. As a sales leader, your commitment to following all the rights shared throughout this book and aligning them with a properly supported company culture will enable you to architect a winning theme for hiring the right people. As a seller, you may not have the power to change the culture at your existing company, but you do have the power to influence it. You also have the power to select a company whose culture best aligns with your potential for success.

The right culture has been and always will be an important facet of my leadership approach. I myself am a strong believer in Maslow Hierarchy of Needs modeling, the value it brings to a business environment, and its ability to uncover the passion of the people within it. In case you are unfamiliar with the model, I will begin by sharing this simplified view of the Maslow Pyramid.

CHART 4: MASLOW HIERARCHY OF NEEDS

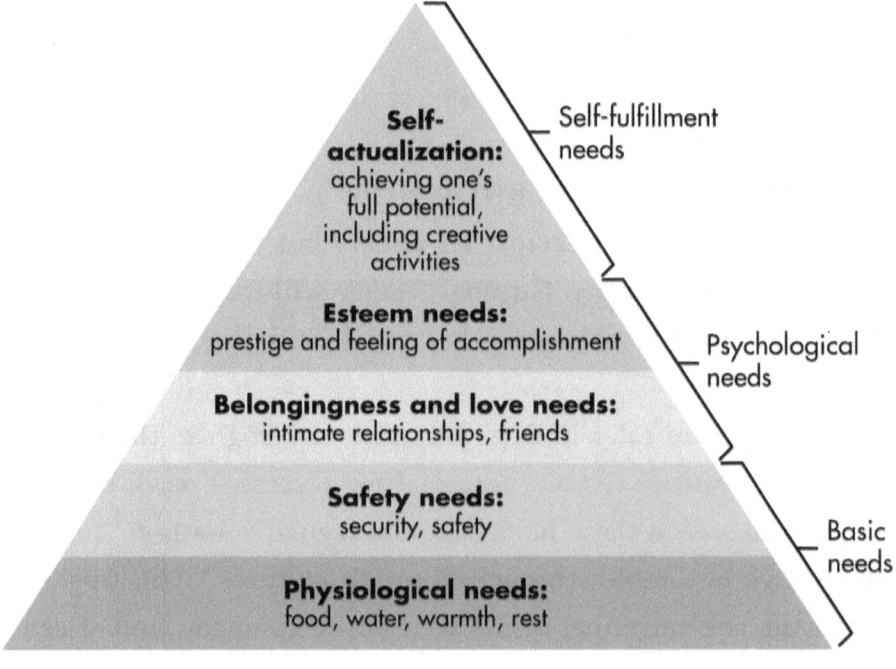

The reason the Maslow Hierarchy of Needs resonates for me is that within its simplicity it has the ability to effectively identify some element of what has meaning for all people in their work environment. I have often said to coworkers that as a leader, I have a responsibility to find the best way of making people wake up in the morning and want to come to work. Making it feel meaningful. I know some will read that last sentence and respond that this is not the leaders' responsibility but the employees'. They get paid, so they should come to work ready to do their job happily. They owe that to the company.

I could not disagree more. Yes, the company pays individuals to work for them, but those skilled individuals can choose to bring their talent anywhere. It is our obligation to earn their commitment by providing an environment and culture that supports a place they aspire to come to each day and aspire to be great. Not just through a paycheck, which has always proven to create at most a temporary commitment to an employer. Think about it: Many of us spend a greater portion of our waking hours at work or thinking about work than we do in our non-working hours' frame of mind. That being the case, I always consider how to create a business environment that touches as many of those Maslow Needs as I possibly can. This has allowed me to run a healthy and inviting environment while delivering a higher level of positive outcomes back to the business—an environment that accelerates the right mindset for achieving greater success for employee and employer.

Again, I am not unaware that the employees have a responsibility here as well. But it is much easier for employees to achieve that balance when they have the benefit of a work environment that is conducive to delivering that positive experience. Both employee and employer own this, and both have a choice. I myself interview candidates for an open position purely based on whether they will or will not be a cultural fit. Their skills matter greatly, but others within the interview team are tasked with reviewing their background, level of skills, and overall qualifications to fulfill the obligations of the role. When I personally sit with candidates, we speak about them, their interests, what they look for in a company, and how they feel the workplace can bring out the best in their abilities. I will be honest; some candidates get uncomfortable with me, as I never even look at their resume while speaking with them. Applying for more senior roles, they believe they have to justify their work experience, yet I always pull them back by asking them to forget about their past roles and tell me more about what matters to you in the work environment. Very rarely, though, do I conclude an interview where the candidate does not thank me for my method and state how refreshing it is not to have to review job after job throughout their career. It's a win-win: This is the first step for them to begin to desire to work on my team or in my company, and now they can see how much their individual needs matter.

But how do I know if my culture is a good fit, if it needs improvement, or what to do to build a good culture? These are all good questions and may differ slightly for all. Let's consider each separately so we can cover them properly.

Is My Company Culture Good Now?

All cultures are different, depending on the company and especially on the expectations of those who work for the company. Sometimes you can sense if a culture is in place and working. Other times you can see it visibly in either a positive or negative way. I will tell you that if your company has not shared with you a defined approach toward having a culture, or numerous employees within the same company cannot seem to align on what the culture might be, a culture most likely exists purely because of the interaction of the employees within the business. This is not unusual, as many companies take culture for granted and live under the philosophy that it takes on a form of its own over time. If a formal plan for defining the culture does not exist, then it is likely not what might be considered a high-performance culture and is at risk of lacking consistency across the business.

Since I am speaking specifically to the individuals within the sales business unit, I will try to focus on that area only. However, any individual business unit culture is most likely influenced by the overarching culture of the broader company as a whole, whether a formal and defined culture exists or not. A business unit can certainly have its own variation of the company culture, but normally that variation does not deviate all too far, especially if the business unit has fewer personnel in proportion to the company base of personnel.

To determine if your culture is positive in a way that can help you achieve all your sales objectives and goals, first gauge your sellers' or sales leaders' job satisfaction. Not if they are happy enough with the money they make or their quotas; those tend to be two areas that are less about culture and more about personal feelings of achievement, and I treat those differently. Are your sellers and sales leaders openly complaining about the work environment, being treated fairly by the company in terms of things like work hours, treatment by other personnel or management, unmet promises, or poor communications throughout the company?

I tend to look for a culture that supports my needs in terms of sales and my approach to how I conduct myself each day. Years ago, I joined a company as Director of sales. The very first day, I participated in my first weekly pipeline review that included all the sales leads across the company and was led by the CEO. My first thought was: *Why does this standard call begin at 6:00 PM?* I tend to treat the evening as employees' quality time with family. My second thought was how odd it was for the CEO to lead the pipeline review. These two points presented immediate cultural inconsistencies for me.

When the call started, my concerns were reinforced. One of our regional sales leaders was discussing their sales expectations for the month, and the CEO cut him off by stating flatly, "You have to be the worst sales leader I have ever hired." Those were his exact words—no exaggeration. Both began screaming at one another, and this type of raised emotion than extended across every sales leader who spoke for the remainder of the call. Once the CEO set that tone, it heightened the stress of anyone who spoke.

Needless to say, the message was clear: this culture was about winning, winning at all costs, and win or you are at risk. For a little while that place was certainly a revolving door of employees coming and going, but after a short period of time that CEO left the organization. Another CEO who cared deeply about culture transitioned into the business, and it began to flourish. An immediate and direct result of the right leadership encouraging the right culture led to both increased revenue and greater employee satisfaction. Not one or the other.

How to Build the Right Culture

Just to be clear, *right* in this situation does not mean that the company simply provides the employees everything they ask for. Right is better defined by a culture that provides you as an employee an environment of shared values and similar beliefs and practices that help bring out your best for your personal success. In most environments, you as a seller or sales leader won't be able to build the culture from scratch, but you will be able to evolve it within your team to make it your own.

The phrase "thank you" increases productivity and motivation beyond imagination, yet not every leader and or executive understands that. Those two words alone begin to define what employees believe to be an existing and strong culture within a company. Why? Because what many employees seek more than anything else is recognition for their efforts, large or small. Of course sellers and sales leaders work hard to earn money, but without the proper level of recognition that begins with something as simple as a thank you, employees begin perceiving that they are in an environment that does not care about or appreciate the hard work they do.

> *A culture that provides you as an employee an environment of shared values and similar beliefs and practices that help bring out your best for your personal success.*

Here is an easy approach to saying thank you in a sales environment that greatly accelerated my business at a company I was leading. Every time we had a win, we celebrated the win in a one-paragraph email distribution that included the names of *all* the team members who supported the engagement. It is important not to overlook supporting team member names on this. No one wants to be left out; this can make them feel as though no one noticed their level of effort, which is a big negative psychologically. I would make the email crisp and concise, mentioned dollar value to gain excitement, and added in to the body of the note statements such as "congratulations," "thank you," "I appreciate," and "your hard work and countless hours of effort," among other things. When I sent it I always included not just the local team but also all the levels of leadership that some of the supporting team reported to directly to assure that those team members could see their direct manager being informed. Additionally, I always included the CEO, COO, president, and SVP of sales.

The result can be highly effective or a complete miss, to be honest. Just doing it is effective as it motivates the individuals named, but what you hope for is that the many individuals who receive the message join in the thread and start a chain reaction of appreciative emails. The successful team really starts to grow in pride as more and more people now see and acknowledge their success. The true winning scenario is when the CEO, COO, president, or SVP of sales also send something as simple as "Great work! Thanks for your efforts." That is when you lock an employee in for at least several weeks of heightened positive energy that often leads to another win or continued fulfillment in the job.

When it can be a miss is when an executive included within the thread simply ignores sending a short but brief appreciation. While executives in particular may feel as though reading it is enough, nothing is more important than taking the 15 seconds or less to respond to it with a thank you. Whether executives think about it or not, those in the thread *always* take note of who was included as a recipient of the email. When they are part of the win and an email goes out, they want to know who received it, as this represents their shining star at that moment. Note to executives: Respond to the email with a thank you. Better yet, for deals deemed significant, pick up the phone to call the team members and say thank you directly.

In a one-on-one discussion with an executive at one company I worked with, he told me that he appreciated the fact that I had started the email chains, especially now that many others were embracing the idea for their own teams, but he hated receiving all the responses. He had asked not to be included in the original email so he would not have to "waste time" filtering all the response emails. I asked him if he did not believe that recognition was part of good leadership. After all, his only duty was to respond with a brief "nice work"—did he not believe that that could change an employee's perspective on the company they work for?

His response was simply: "It's annoying to have to do, and I do not have time. I think those emails are so corny." Let me add that during the years I worked in that company, that leader had not achieved his numbers for the business unit he led and had frequent issues of employee dissatisfaction. He was ultimately moved to a role where he did not have sellers working for him. This was the only issue I've ever run into with the congratulations emails.

The regularity of the communication, the level of information shared, and the general understanding that all employees value that knowledge helps inform this style of acknowledgment. That knowledge often becomes their perception of who the leadership and company as a whole. The environments where I have seen the highest levels of employee satisfaction are those in which the executive team communicated well within the business. This is not to say that they shared their innermost secrets, but the executives who understand that information is power and a sign of respect tend to lead an environment where the culture is strong. Communications might include such things as a monthly all-hands call from the executives, a quarterly review of financial and business outcomes, or regular email communications sharing a business decision, and all help inform and engage employees. Environments that suffer are those where employees have uncertainty or inconsistent information flow from what is more a rumor mill than direct executive engagement.

Invest in culture, develop your culture and your people, and welcome an environment of openness toward improvement and innovation. I have primarily worked within environments that are based on technology, so I am used to sellers and sales leaders who want to be expressive and who cultivate many ideas for creativity. That is one of the very reasons they and I expect that many people choose to work for a company: They want to have a voice and company who listens to the value of their input. This is not to say that the company always acts on those ideas, but the ability for employees to share ideas or be given the opportunity to participate in teams that allow their voice to come out is a culture most aspire to be a part of.

> *Invest in culture, develop your culture and your people, and welcome an environment of openness toward improvement and innovation.*

Another important facet of a culture is the commitment the company and broader base of employees make to abiding by its values. One of the most frustrating things for employees, either in a sales capacity or supporting a selling structure, is being in a sales environment that says yes to every request because the customer asked for it rather than saying no when it is better and smarter to say no. This is especially true if and when those very sellers, sales leaders, and supporting personnel provide feedback stating the company should not pursue or work the engagement and yet it is determined by someone (often executives) that it should be pursued regardless. This is a quick conflict with the right strategy and right solutions mindset I suggest for success.

Consider in a technical selling world an example of why your success is impacted when you deviate from cultural values for a particular deal. A prospective customer asks your company to bid on an RFP. Your sellers and technical personnel review the details of the RFP. The seller clearly wants to pursue it, but the technical personnel have clearly identified the various elements of the RFP that the company cannot do, as the skills or capabilities are not aligned to its defined business capabilities. Additionally, your assessment shows that there exists only a small potential to win the engagement. Executives have decided, though, regardless of the experts' input, that we should work it anyway. After all, we need the sale and potential for revenue regardless of the likelihood of winning.

I use this as an example of culture because it is more common than not in technology sales environments. Why is it under right culture and not something I share under right solution or right customer? Because when you have a team of individuals who have committed into the defined values and culture the business declares they live by, yet the answer to a poorly qualified deal is to work it because we need the sale and revenue regardless of their opinions, it is contradictory to the reasons people originally bought into the culture. As sellers and sales leaders, we get it: Companies care about money, and money is the reason employees get paid. But if a culture is defined by having the right people and the right solutions and yet in the heat of the battle the revenue is foremost, the values your culture was built on begin to crumble in the minds of those employees who once believed you were committed to something different. Companies have to appreciate why this happens.

I have been known to use the example of the technical engineer who has to respond to many of the technical responses within the RFP we mentioned earlier. This technical engineer has to work all day to keep customers happy, but also has to fit in responding to an RFP, which we all know happens all too frequently after hours—the engineer's personal time with family. Now, how will that individual feel about the culture within their company if they have already told the company this RFP was poorly defined and not an RFP we are capable of winning? How will that individual feel when answering questions in that RFP late into the evening, potentially every evening for several weeks, rather than spending time with their family or just spending priceless time reading a book or relaxing? They worked a 10-hour workday, and now they are addressing a poorly qualified RFP for 3-4 hours a night. I promise you that the mood of that individual and their sustainable commitment to the company culture is now waning. This is different, by the way, from those times the technical engineer occasionally has to work evening hours on a deal where people feel strongly that we can win. The mood and commitment is far different there. They still are not pleased to use family time to do the work, but in their heart and mind they at least believe it will have a positive impact and that it is worth the time to do the work.

Sellers and sales leaders are no different than most employees. They have an option of which company they choose to work for. In return, they want confidence in the fact that their executive team has the right strategic plan for their success, applies the right leadership to lead the effort, and has the right people and supporting cast to help them achieve their goals. They want all this while enjoying a company that has the right culture that is conducive to a healthy environment they can be proud to represent to the right customers.

Culture can be a significant differentiator for sellers and sales leaders. One of the most valuable parts of the success a company achieves with its customers and partners, culture can neither be overlooked nor underestimated for the value it provides to your outcomes.

Chapter 16

THE TIME IS RIGHT NOW
Success That Waits Is Success Lost

"Don't wait: The time will never be just right."
Napoleon Hill

HOW MANY TIMES HAVE YOU HEARD someone in the leadership levels of your company say "Let's wait until the next fiscal year" before initiating a much-needed change within the business?

I will be honest: I am that guy who will assuredly say in response, "Why? The change will add value today!" Not in an attempt to be challenging or defiant, but as a true commitment to achieve the strategic goals that have been established right away. In my view, if you recognize as leaders that a change will be beneficial to the success of your business and you see that that change will lead to increased business improvements, then tell me again why you should wait! If those improvements are real and we accept that they will be beneficial, you will only delay success or miss it entirely by waiting.

I recognize that I said *if those improvements are real*. Obviously, we want to ensure that changes are necessary and confirm that the expected outcomes normally turn out that way. I will give you an example. I was working in a leadership capacity for one company, and by just the second month of the new fiscal year I had mathematically proven that the compensation modeling for a specialized area of the business was incorrectly defined, resulting in a high likelihood that millions in potential revenue would be at risk. That risk, by the way, would cost the company earnings not just within the current fiscal year, but also in the following fiscal year. It took until the fifth month of the fiscal year to have the executive team agree and accept that a mistake was made.

Think about what I just said. The executives were told that a multi-million-dollar error had been uncovered, and it took three more months for them to even acknowledge that the error existed. And even then, although I had clear documentation that the error was going to negatively impact the remainder of the fiscal year for both company and sales personnel as well as place part of the following fiscal year's success at risk, I was told that the change would need to wait until the next fiscal year when new plans were created. A potential loss of millions in new sales revenue and tens of thousands in lost commission for sales personnel—and we should *wait another seven months* to implement the change? The error could have been corrected with nine months remaining in the fiscal year, thus potentially protecting the millions of dollars at risk—and yet the decision was to wait. What does that say to me as an employee? It's better to wait until it's more convenient, rather than act to protect the sellers' ability to be successful and the welfare of the company as a whole. Why do things like this occur?

Of course, in all the examples I use, special conditions might apply and should be considered. But *considered* to me means that we should consider the best way to remediate and implement the change now, when value can be recognized, not consider how long we can delay so as not to upset current "finalized" fiscal year planning. Doing things because they are easier, not because they are logical, strikes me as the most significant determiner of why change does or does not take place. I cannot agree that doing what is easy always equals good leadership when it is clearly the wrong choice and will have negative ramifications. When a change is recognized as one that will benefit the success of a business, good leaders act. Nothing should stand in the way of that success, especially something so unimportant as an annual planning tradition.

The beginning of a fiscal year has and will always be most companies' chance to redefine their strategic approach for the coming year's business success. Company-wide, the business units begin to evaluate the past year's success and those changes and or tweaks that will best lead to the coming year's success. It is a great opportunity to evaluate, define, and implement new processes and strategies, and when done properly, should help employees reach the highest levels of success across the business. Not only do I agree with the rationale of the process, it is one of my favorite times of the year. Other than winning a deal, I find nothing more fulfilling than defining a well-thought-out strategy, driving the plan into action, and seeing it achieve the defined goals. For a strategy to work, it must be applied harmoniously across the entire business—every business unit and sales methodology—and all the elements of each compensation model must be balanced to ensure it is driving toward a common goal.

But if we demonstrate that much commitment to our plans and apply the necessary rigor to make them reach the highest possible level of success, why would we as sellers or sales leaders allow any foreseen risk or known miscalculation place them in jeopardy? The expectation as sellers and sales leaders is to attain your goals, no exceptions. So why would you allow your success be put on hold when you can clearly see room for an improvement? You would not, because you are committed sellers and sales leaders.

Now, do not equate what I have discussed as business risk related to miscalculation to a deviation from the defined strategy. They are not the same. I firmly believe in not deviating from a defined strategy, as doing so can place your business success at risk. The discussion of the miscalculation was not a strategy change; it was a financial correction to part of the strategic planning that was incorrectly calculated and would result in us missing the defined strategic goals. Another example of this would be when a seller has a customer who wants to purchase a product or service from their company, yet that product or service is not currently part of the company's existing business capabilities. The seller knows, however, that the company is planning to add that offering in the next 12 months, so is pushing the company to add it now so as to not miss the potential for new sales revenue. That would be a change in strategy; adding the offering before the company is properly prepared in the best way possible would carry a high risk of negative repercussions. Such deviations from the strategic direction of the business should be avoided.

My recommendation is to continually inspect all aspects of your business to assure that your plans, people, and processes are working optimally. Be vigilant and expect no less from others you rely on for success, including your executive team members. Your success is their success, so challenge everything worth challenging if it can lead to increased success—but do so only if it poses no risk to the customer or your company.

Consider your overall plan for success and the timing you need to apply it as no different than the value of time when it comes to individual deals and customer engagement. Each of you have experience in sales or the activity related to the sales process; thus all of you understand the value and importance in acting swiftly when it comes to engaging with customers and pursuing deals that satisfy their needs. Many customer needs are planned, while others are unplanned and require immediate assistance. Either is a potential for you as a seller or sales leader to enable your business to stand out above the competition, but in doing so, time is of the essence.[3]

Know that success for sellers and sales leaders is out there every day if they can manage time properly. In business we have little ability to wait in responding to customers, and an "I will get to it tomorrow" mentality can and often will open the door to competitors. I worked for years as a Cisco reseller. There is nothing that better exemplified the importance of time for me than the knowledge that Cisco had no less than 1,000 competitors in the very region I supported. Consider how many minutes there are in every day, and how few of those minutes it takes to allow a competitor to beat you to the sale. Consider how many times in your career you have spoken with a customer and were told a decision had already been made; think about what might have been had you just called earlier that day or the day before.

Regretting the past is a waste of time, and anxiety will steal energy from the future. Focus on right now. Move mindfully with speed and quality, and make it count.

---

[3] What has to be tempered is the urge to create a sense of unnecessary urgency in all situations. This is also a timing balance issue, more in respect to how you engage and work internal to your business, but it is also important to your success. Your resources can easily become disenchanted with you if urgency is incorrectly applied. Few people want to be pushed to get requests done now simply because they are important to you. As time passes, your own resource pool could begin to lose faith in you and lack a desire to support your requests.

Chapter 17

REAPING THE BENEFITS FROM THE RIGHT RESULTS
A Lifetime of Success

BENEFITS IN SALES CAN COME in many forms. Most sellers and sales leaders recognize the financial rewards that come from excelling at achieving their goals. Money is the very reason many people get into sales initially, and it often becomes the addiction that keeps them coming back for more. So what could be more intoxicating than aligning with a methodology that leads to even greater achievements on a more consistent basis? My methodology will never replace the need for hard work in addition to properly applying the model in a way that benefits you personally. One without the other will no doubt limit your potential.

Financial benefits, either professional or personal, are really just one aspect of the rewards you stand to reap from following these methods. As I often instruct my teams and the groups I speak with, financial rewards extend to benefit life beyond your bank account. Consider the following as a result of your efforts:

1. Business earnings for your personal life
2. Financial achievement for your business environment
3. Financial sustainability
4. Financial security
5. Working for a company with an aligned and balanced culture
6. Higher levels of recognition and reward within your company
7. Increased confidence
8. Expanded potential for career growth
9. Expanded potential for network growth
10. Reputation for being a top performer along with the respect that follows within your work environment
11. Improved quality of life with greater potential for increased family time
12. Job and career satisfaction

Only you know what matters most in terms of the benefits you hope to receive. Over my 30 years of sales and sales leadership, I can tell you that I have seen the highs and the lows. Thankfully, the highs have far exceeded and outlasted the lows. But the lows are of great benefit and equally important to experience. If you lose and learn nothing from it, you have missed one of the most important lessons of your success path. That's right: losing is one of the most valuable benefits you can ever experience in the world of sales.

Obviously, I don't recommend that you intentionally go out and lose a deal; that's neither the point nor sales smart. But you will never learn how to win and win better and more often unless you also learn how loss happens and how it feels. When

> **You will never learn how to win and win better and more often unless you also learn how loss happens and how it feels.**

it does, pay attention and study it. With luck, it will sicken you so much that you will have a heightened yet controlled sense of awareness the next time around. Let's face it. Losing sucks—in business, sports, and all aspects of your life—but losing does create a different level of strength that aids us in creating a repeatable ability to succeed time and time again. So while I do not recommend losing often, I do recommend you embrace it when it occurs, as it will eventually help you reach the goals you have defined for yourself. Honestly, if a loss does not hurt, then you do not care enough to be in a sales career in the first place; if you ignore the lesson it teaches you, then you have no idea what opportunity for greater achievement looks like. Either way, maybe sales is not your career path, as good sellers see and experience both.

My approach to sales and sales leadership has worked soundly for my and my team's success for years. I trust my models implicitly. While my confidence is high in that regard, the success you experience could differ. Remember, I have strong beliefs in how I run my business, and have had the good fortune to select companies that allow me the opportunity to drive my own initiatives. Your outcome will in some part depend on your situation, but I have no doubt that if you continue and apply my methodology wherever possible, it will bring you success.

The rights work for me because I use them in unison and never overlook or neglect the importance of each. As a reminder, let me share again the attainment to quota tables and charts I discussed earlier in "Chapter 14: The Right Quota or Budget." When you do not apply all your rights as a seller or sales leader to the highest level of potential, you continue to risk or place unnecessary burden on your ability to achieve your goals. Every choice you make has a positive or negative impact. You have the power to instill more positives than negatives.

I have added the charts as a quick visual reminder of how your success could be impacted now that you have completed the reading.

CHART 5: RIGHT CHOICES

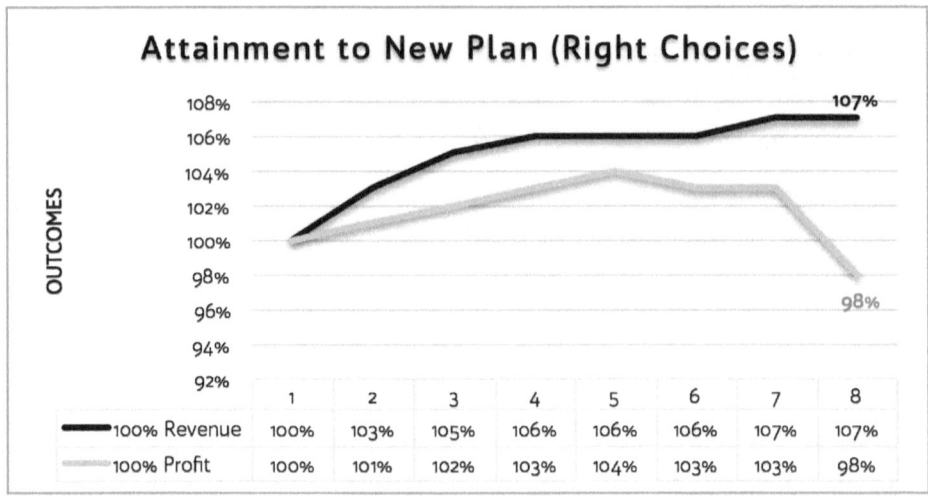

CHART 6: STATUS QUO

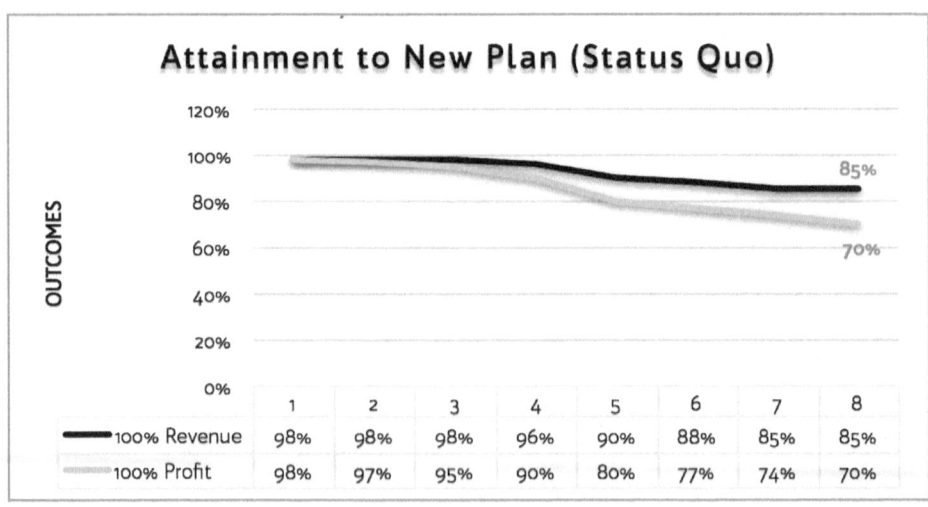

I won't state my points related to the charts again to the depth previously discussed in Chapter 14. What I will offer is a question that you as sellers and sales leader may want to ask yourselves: If you have the responsibility and power to control your own outcomes, would you rather stand in front of your executive team with the results of Chart 5 or Chart 6? From experience, I will tell you that Chart 5 is a much easier and comfortable discussion. It offers the potential of career progression, increased reputation throughout the business, and improved opportunity to maximize your financial attainment. Just as important, your executive team will look at you with a sense of confidence and trust. The discussion that will occur related to Chart 6 will lead to an extensive list of questions, frustration, and open concerns about whether you can live up to the expectations of the role.

It is within your power to take control of the results you achieve, the benefits you can receive, and the way you are perceived by those you interact with.

Chapter 18

YOUR NEW PATH TO IMPROVING SUCCESS

Turning Lessons into Practice

THIS FINAL CHAPTER IS YOUR ENCOURAGEMENT to use some, if not all, of the principles I have shared that continue to lead to my success. I would be remiss if I did not state again that my best success was recognized when I followed all of the rights, not some. They work best for me as a complete solution, not as pieces. Consider that when you know with confidence in your mind and heart what leads to the best outcome for you, as the rights have given me, each element individually will lead to some improvement—but the greater achievement is to apply them as an entire model to gain their full benefits.

It has taken me years of learning to find an approach that worked best for me and my teams, and when you apply it with the right level of commitment, I am confident your success in sales will prosper. I have never been a fan of believing that one size fits all. I remind you that the methods worked for me because I was able to make all the rights work well collectively and overcome the traditional concerns others tend to have when a transformation or change model is being applied. Patience can without a doubt be a virtue during this evolution, and the more confidence you have, even in the toughest of times, the better you can help others overcome their stress during this time. Just know that emotions will be heightened while you lead other team members to greener pastures, and you will need to have the ability to persevere.

I do believe that these principles are sound and will work for anyone who believes in their possibilities, but your ability to get the most out of them will be based on how well you make small tweaks to employ them properly in your business environment. This is no different than how every company has a vision, mission, strategic plan, and a plethora of business plans, but they all differ according to many factors. Only you can fully understand the most effective blend of these rights for your situation.

Before we close, I want to mention a word that I have avoided using throughout this book: *instinct*. I would be lying if I did not say that my instincts come into play when making choices. However, I utilize my instincts only when all my rights have been applied and I know the role those instincts can play in enhancing the decision-making process. Instincts can make a difference to an experienced seller or sales leader, and when applied alongside the rights defined in this book, can provide a valuable edge towards your success. Instinct, however, is something learned through experience. That experience comes from years of losing when you thought you might win and winning when you thought you might lose and all the people and processes that play a role along the way. I have cited many of my favorite quotations throughout this book; in terms of instinct and intuition, my feelings are best summed up by the anonymous quote "Trust your instincts; intuition doesn't lie."

But while I am a believer in instincts in the decision-making process, I hold greater faith in what my instincts are telling me when they are properly supported and validated by good information and data. I do feel that intuition can lie, as it can be based on emotion and emotions are driven from the heart. We all know from our personal lives that emotions can lead us down incorrect paths if not properly validated; consider what emotions can do when you have been waiting to earn a commission for months or your job feels like it is on the line. Your intuition can be a great value toward your success, but it can also be misread every once in a while. I have spoken throughout this book about being honest with yourself, and I believe strongly you should listen to your instincts but know when to question them in times of duress.

Your instinct to pick up this book was correct, as will be your decision (I hope) to apply the rights to your own personal methods of selling or sales leadership. I hope this information was a useful tool, and that it has helped you to gain what you were looking for when you purchased the book.

Go win, succeed, and have fun!

8 RIGHTS FOR SUCCESS

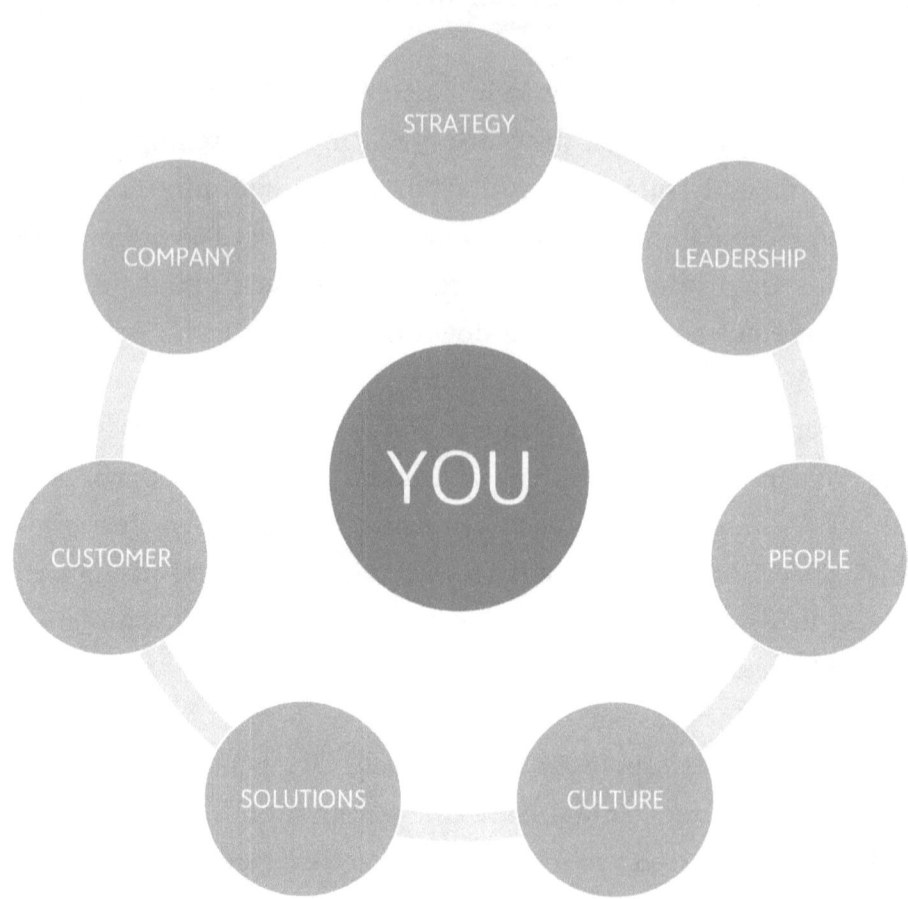

MIKE CONNOLLY is an accomplished innovator in the practice of sales strategy and business execution. He has built a successful career in sales, sales management, and sales operations. His leadership has helped generate billions of dollars in new revenue over his 30-year career. It is through his career experiences that he developed critical skills in generating consistent overachievement of selling outcomes for both sales personnel and their organizations.

Amidst it all, he has earned his Master of Business Administration (MBA) from the Duke University Fuqua School of Business, while also being a devoted husband and father.

www.ingramcontent.com/pod-product-compliance
Lightning Source LLC
Chambersburg PA
CBHW021422170526
45164CB00001B/55